The Beauty of What Remains

"The wisdom Steve Leder shares in this moving book is an essential part of living a beautiful and meaningful life. Read it and feel inspired."
                                                              —Maria Shriver

"With *The Beauty of What Remains*, Rabbi Leder has given us a profoundly thoughtful book that captures the same wisdom and wit that his congregation has experienced from him for over three decades. Give this book to a friend."   —Aaron Sorkin

"Rabbi Leder has a way of making us all feel better, even when tackling the difficult subject of death. I was underlining and dog-earing from the start. Life lessons on each page."   —Hoda Kotb

"Rabbi Steve Leder's wise and kind voice gently guides us through his life with his father as well as the lives of so many others he has helped. His personal history makes him and his work so accessible and satisfying. This warm and insightful book teaches us how to remember what really matters in loss and in life."
                                —David Kessler, author of *Finding Meaning:*
                                                   The Sixth Stage of Grief

"Rabbi Steve Leder writes about grief and pain in *The Beauty of What Remains*—but also about the joy and love we can find in the most unexpected places. This gorgeous book will provide comfort to many."   —Jenna Bush Hager

"I've changed my will because of this book. I don't necessarily mean the will with instructions for the disposition of my earthly possessions. I mean the will composed not by a lawyer but by my life, the legacy of the love, the values, the virtues that make life worth living. A life lived like that can create beauty even in the valley of the shadow of death. I cried, I laughed, and my heart sang—now, death, where is your sting? Thank you, Rabbi Leder, for sharing your will with us."

—Bishop Michael Curry, author of *Love Is the Way*

"Steve Leder's words are a balm to the soul. *The Beauty of What Remains* encourages us to confront our feelings about death head-on, and reminds us not to fear the end of life on Earth, but to embrace what it can teach us while we're here. Steve's own stories and experiences are written in that exquisite way that makes it feel as if you're speaking to a good friend. This book is a must-read."

—Mallika Chopra, author of *Living with Intent: My Somewhat Messy Journey to Purpose, Peace, and Joy*

"Through numerous recollections of conversing with the dying, Rabbi Steve Leder takes the reader on a transformational journey providing insights and caring support in releasing all fear of death and really living a meaningful life. I highly recommend this book, particularly for those who are grieving the loss of a loved one."

—Anita Moorjani, *New York Times*–bestselling author of *Dying to Be Me* and *What If This Is Heaven?*

"An exquisite book on the deepest truth we will all face. I whole-heartedly recommend."

—Roshi Joan Jiko Halifax, author of *Being with Dying*

The Beauty

of

What Remains

HOW OUR GREATEST FEAR
BECOMES OUR GREATEST GIFT

Steve Leder

AVERY
an imprint of Penguin Random House
New York

AVERY

an imprint of Penguin Random House LLC
penguinrandomhouse.com

First trade paperback edition 2023

The Library of Congress has cataloged the hardcover edition of this book as follows:

Names: Leder, Steven Z., author.
Title: The beauty of what remains: how our greatest
fear becomes our greatest gift / Steve Leder.
Description: New York: Avery, 2021.
Identifiers: LCCN 2020026855 (print) | LCCN 2020026856 (ebook) |
ISBN 9780593187555 (hardcover) | ISBN 9780593187562 (ebook)
Subjects: LCSH: Death. | Terminally ill. | Conduct of life.
Classification: LCC HQ1073.L437 2021 (print) |
LCC HQ1073 (ebook) | DDC 306.9—dc23
LC record available at https://lccn.loc.gov/2020026855
LC ebook record available at https://lccn.loc.gov/2020026856

ISBN (paperback) 9780593421376

Printed in the United States of America
1st Printing

Book design by Laura K. Corless

To my parents,
Leonard and Barbara Leder

CONTENTS

My first funeral as a rabbi was for a twenty-five-year-old named Ricky who died of AIDS-related illness. I was twenty-seven, fresh out of the seminary, earnest, eager even, as I knocked on the door of the modest home of his parents, Joe and Irena, for what clergy call an "intake" meeting. Joe led me to the Formica kitchen table, where he and Irena sat beside two cups of cold black coffee and a dirty ashtray. Eyes swollen, tired and wary, they smoked in silence and sized me up. I offered some platitudes and the obligatory "I'm so sorry." Then I noticed the tattooed numbers on their left arms—Auschwitz. They smoked and stared a little longer until I broke the silence to ask about Ricky. Irena answered each question with a few words, took a drag, and waited for the next. Joe said nothing. They were each suspended in some distant, surreal dimension of time. Broken long ago, they were broken again, their suffering commingled with ash. Such a young, inexperienced rabbi, only two years older than their dead son. I must have seemed yet another insult to their injury. They knew, and I knew, I had nothing to offer and nothing to say.

During my more than three decades tending to more than a thousand grieving families since that afternoon, I have learned a lot about death, which in turn has taught me a lot about life. Two years ago, I decided to share my insights about the ways death gives meaning to life with my congregation in a sermon delivered on the eve of Yom Kippur, the holiest day of the Jewish year. That sermon on death turned out to be the most popular sermon I have ever delivered from the pulpit.

I chose the theme of death and what it teaches us about life because in addition to being a day devoted to seeking forgiveness from those we have wronged, Yom Kippur has built into it several observances meant to mimic death. It is a day of fasting because the dead neither eat nor drink. We wear white as a reminder of the white linen burial shroud. The service begins with a lengthy prayer chanted three times in succession while facing three sacred scrolls, representing the three judges that legend has it each of us will face in the heavenly tribunal. Many of the prayers that day allude to death in one way or another. One of those prayers hauntingly asks, "Who shall live and who shall die?" The answer for each of us is "I will."

We end Yom Kippur afternoon with the very same words that Jewish tradition requires us to recite when a person dies. The idea behind these rituals and prayers is the hope that contemplating death will inspire us to change our lives.

The sermon was what preachers call a "list" sermon, in which I listed and then elaborated upon ten lessons I had learned about death as a result of seeing it up close for so many years. Requests for copies poured in from all over the world. That's when I knew I would write this book. What I didn't know was that my father would be buried one year to the day after that sermon was delivered and that his death would force me to rethink both my sermon and this book. Yes, when I wrote the sermon, I definitely knew more than the day I knocked on Joe and Irena's door. But just when I thought I really knew something, my dad, much as he had done so many times before in his life, pushed me painfully further in death. Lenny Leder had incredible instincts born of his youth on the streets. My entire life I hated it when he would say, "Steven, where you are, I've been. You don't know shit." My father's death forced me to realize that what I knew about death and how it informs life was the result of seeing other families' loved ones die—other families' grief, not mine. Sure, I had seen a lot of loss, but vicariously, one degree removed from the truth. I was an experienced rabbi well-schooled in the craft of death. But my dad was right—I was full of shit.

This book is my apology—setting the record straight for the ways in which that most popular sermon was shy of the deepest truth. I want people to know the deepest truth about what death teaches us of life. I want us all to lead more meaningful, more beautiful lives; less anxious, less frenetic. I am writing this prologue after twelve weeks of stay-at-home orders. Pandemic death has caused the greatest global pause in our history. Death has the potential to change us and to change the world because it reveals the depth of our love for one another and for life itself. Understanding death—its rituals, its lessons, its gift to reshape love through memory, its grief, its powerful reminder that it is not what but who we have that matters—gives our lives exquisite meaning. I still write in part as a rabbi, but this time as a rabbi forced, as nearly all sons and daughters eventually are, to make peace with the loss, love, regret, and pain that result from the death of a father.

The first time I felt how painfully complicated it would be for me—the rabbi and the son—to face my father's slow decline was the first Friday afternoon he spent in a nursing home. The home was established by the Jewish community in Minneapolis to take care of its elderly. It was a Friday afternoon, and knowing who I was, the program director asked if I would please lead the brief weekly service in the activities room for the residents to welcome the Sabbath. Then she handed me an inflated balloon.

"What's this for?" I asked.

"Well," she said, "it's good for the residents to have a little exercise and stimulation during the service. All you need to do is hit the balloon toward them in their wheelchairs, and when one of them catches the balloon, it's that person's turn to answer a question, sing with you, clap their hands, or do whatever else you want them to do to participate in the service. It helps them stay engaged."

On my father's first day in a nursing home, I got up in that cheerless multipurpose room full of old, confused souls and put on my best rabbi act. I was outgoing, full of wisecracks, and loud; I exaggerated my gestures, much as I did most Friday mornings at services for the temple's nursery school children back home. The same shtick worked equally well in both places. I hit the balloon and watched it drift toward the twenty or so residents on my father's floor, all gathered together, many unsure why. "Good catch, Sally! Now, help me with the blessing for the candles. That's it. Come on. You know the words. Okay, it's coming to you next, Morrie. Attaboy, arms up. Grab it. Good job! Now, sing with me, Morrie. Come on, clap your hands too . . ."

For reasons and in ways you will understand later, my dad

was not like other dads. The idea of playing a game with my father or his catching a balloon or participating in anything with a group was hard to imagine. I had never in my entire life played a single game of catch with my dad. We never shot baskets together in the driveway; not once did we toss a baseball or a football around in the yard. But there he was, my formerly strong, uncompliant, difficult, powerful, frightening, hilarious, crude, successful dad, in a wheelchair in a nursing home, lined up with the listless and the lost, his arms in the air, hoping for a balloon. How could it be?

I didn't want to toss him the balloon. I didn't want to make him part of my act. But he was waiting, like the rest of his new neighbors, for the rabbi to send the magical floating orb his way. So I did. He caught it and smiled a little. "That's great, Dad. Now, clap your hands with me . . ."

That first afternoon in the nursing home, my dad actually played a game with me—his arms aloft, welcoming something offered to him by his son, bittersweetly, with regret and love. I finished the service, walked into the hallway, shuddered, and wept. I had begun the journey from rabbi to son— from all that death takes away to the beauty of what remains.

1

The Deepest Peace

All the rivers run into the sea, and yet the sea is not full.
To the place from which the rivers come,
there they return again.

—ECCLESIASTES 1:7

We were a small group, most of us a year out of college and just back from Israel, where we had spent the first of our five-year curriculum learning Hebrew. Now that we were stateside, it was time to learn everything else required to serve our pulpits and keep our tradition alive. That included a field trip to death's storefront, the mortuary. Looking at the shallow, twin-bed-sized porcelain table on stainless-steel legs with a drain toward the bottom and a coiled hose above, I realized that I would have to face a lot of death in my career. You'd think I would have figured that out before I entered the seminary, but then again, how many people who decide what they want to be at fifteen really think things through? "This is where we wash and prepare the bodies," the mortician said matter-of-factly. He went on to describe what happened from the moment he arrived at a home or hospital to retrieve a body to the moment a family drove away from the gravesite, leaving their loved one buried beneath the earth.

That porcelain platform for washing and prepping, the casket showroom and the little signs with prices, the book of flower arrangements and the makeup room shocked me. I had been to only one funeral in my life: my grandmother's. I was seven years old. The only thing I remember was my auntie Geta crying in a way I had never heard anyone cry before. My classmates and I made a lot of sick jokes as we moved from room to room. But there was no denying death was going to be a regular part of my life, so I had a lot to learn.

I became a rabbi for a lot of both simple and complicated reasons. My father and uncle owned a junkyard, where I worked hard as a kid. Hard work was the only thing that seemed to get my father's attention; it was what he expected and what he valued. Any creative pursuit for which I showed potential—writing, music, acting—was summarily dismissed as frivolous. Sports were laughable. And my young mother, Barbara, over-burdened as she was with five kids, made it clear when we were very young that she wasn't the carpooling, den mother, team mom sort of mother other kids on the block had. It was all she could do to feed us, keep the house clean, and manage the doctor and dentist appointments and parent-teacher conferences. If we wanted to do anything extra, we were on our own. With one exception—the synagogue.

Because Lenny Leder grew up in the Jewish ghetto of North Minneapolis, Jewish culture was all he knew, and as far as he was concerned, it was the only culture that mattered. My childhood was filled with Yiddish, sour pickles, bagels and smoked fish on Sunday mornings, and little care or contact with the larger world. If I wanted to play hockey or baseball, act in the school play, or write for the school paper, I had to figure out how to do that for myself, and there weren't going to be any pats on the back if I did. But if I wanted a ride to the synagogue to attend the youth group, Dad and therefore Mom were all in. It seemed as if anything I did at the synagogue made them proud and little if anything I did elsewhere other than sweating it out at the junkyard was even noticed. You don't have to be Sigmund Freud to understand why I became a rabbi.

When I was fourteen, I was smoking pot at school most days, failing algebra and Spanish, playing drums in a rock band, and heading for trouble. While my parents were away on vacation, my bandmates and I came up with the bright idea to steal some Bob Dylan albums from the local Target. We got caught by an undercover security guard and ended up at the police station, where my oldest sister had to pick me up and take me home until my parents returned from Florida for the meeting with the detective. I was the fourth of five children, and I think my parents were sort of over being parents by the time I and my little brother came around. The arrest was a warning to them that some oversight might be in order. Wary of psychologists, they went to our rabbi for counsel. He told them he thought what I needed was a change of peers and suggested they send me to a Jewish summer camp in Oconomowoc, Wisconsin. It was there I fell deeply in love. I loved the music, I loved the cool, guitar-playing hippie counselors. I loved the pretty girls from Chicago with flowers in their hair. It was the first time in my life I ever saw a rabbi in shorts and a T-shirt who could throw a baseball. It was a revelation to me that rabbis could be just like normal people yet also seem to possess a special, wise secret worthy of respect. That summer I knew that when I grew up, I wanted to be like them.

It was the beginning of a twelve-year journey toward ordination, at the end of which the fifteen-year-old in me was sure I would spend my time making camp as great for my future congregation's kids as it was for me. I would study and teach Talmud. I would write inspiring sermons, read and write wonderful books, and ponder the great mystery that is life itself. Standing in front of that autopsy and embalming table was my first indication that I was heading for something else too. It left me quietly, secretly, afraid.

Even after finishing my studies I remained afraid of dying and of death. One tour of a mortuary notwithstanding, rabbinical school had prepared me poorly for both. But I was fortunate enough to have a great mentor in the then-senior rabbi of my first congregation, where I have stayed my entire career and now serve as the senior rabbi myself. My first week on the job he took me with him to watch an unveiling ceremony. These ceremonies take place roughly a year after the burial and involve a few prayers followed by the unveiling of the headstone marking the grave. After leading the requisite prayers, the rabbi asked the widow to lift the cloth covering from the headstone. Instantly, she broke into sobs the likes of which I had not heard since my auntie Geta's at my grandmother's funeral—primal, uncontrollable, inconsolable, pent-up pain.

"I can't," she wailed.

I was paralyzed. My boss wasn't. He put his arm around her shoulder and said, "You can. Get control of yourself. Your children and grandchildren are here. That's it. Good . . ."

I watched in amazement as she stepped forward and lifted the cloth covering, revealing her husband's legacy carved into stone. I saw that people can and do face death and grief even when they think they can't. I never would have believed it at the time, but I have become much like my first boss and that funeral director whose tour shocked me with its matter-of-factness long ago. From years of experience, they understood that death really is a part of life—essential, universal, expected, mundane even. None of us are making history when we die, and in many ways, all our deaths are the same. I understand that now too.

Thirty-some years after that rabbinical school mortuary tour I am with my mother at the funeral home in Minneapolis. My father is deep into Alzheimer's, and ever the planner, my mother wants to make arrangements. The guy in charge knows his stuff, and after my mom introduces me as her son who's a rabbi in Los Angeles, he knows the same is true of me. We work our way through the checklist: type of casket; flowers for the casket spray; guestbook yes, video montage no; military honors no, Freemason honors yes; burial shroud no, prayer shawl yes. Music? "Mom, we gotta go with Hank Williams." Limo yes. I was glad that I could help my mom that day; that I had become a death professional who knew the behind-the-scenes machinations of it all. I was trying my best to be a rabbi and a son. And the truth is, if I had not had on the armor of my profession that day, if I had been only the son whose father was soon going to die, I am not sure what I would have done with so much sadness.

I had never spoken with my dad about what he wanted for his funeral, but I had asked him, a couple of years before this, if he was afraid of dying. I chose that particular visit with my dad to ask him if he was afraid, because I felt it was coming to the end of the time when he could still comprehend questions and respond with a nod, yes or no. The rabbi and the son in me wanted to ease whatever worry or fear he might have had at the time about what was happening to him. "Dad, you got a lot right," I told him. "I am a success because you taught me how to work harder than anyone else, and that has made all the difference." It was true. Other rabbis had higher SAT scores, know more Talmud, and speak better Hebrew than I do. But none I know of outwork me. Thank you, Dad.

"Dad? This isn't the hardest thing you have ever been through, is it?" I asked next. He shook his head no. "Was the worst thing you ever went through when your parents stopped talking to you because you and Uncle Mort left your dad's junkyard to start your own?" He nodded yes. "Then you can deal with this too, right?" Again, he nodded yes. As a rabbi now experienced in helping people through their suffering, I knew reminding people facing something difficult that they have faced difficulties before and found a way through helps them face their current challenges too. After that brief exchange, he stared blankly into the distance. He was like that now—here for a moment, then gone. I was trying my best to be his rabbi and his son during what I believed might well be the last back-and-forth of our lives.

After more than thirty years, I have visited nearly a thousand dying people, and so far not one—not one single person who is really, actively dying—has told me he or she was afraid. In fact, most people summon me to their bedside because they want to speak fearlessly and openly about their death, their funeral; what they want me to say and not to say. A family sometimes asks me to visit with their dying loved one because they are afraid of life without them or they assume their loved one is panicked, but the agenda of the dying is not one of fear, it is one of peace. Often the first thing a dying person says after thanking me for coming is "I'm fine." And they mean it.

Lionel was ninety-two years old when he called and asked me to visit. His wife, Terry, had died three years before. She was a beautiful person. We often say when someone has died, "May her memory be a blessing." For most, it's just an expression. For Terry, it was a profound truth, a powerful statement about the way she lived and loved. To know her, to be with her, to have her in your corner, in your life, in your heart and memory—this really was a blessing. Anyone who knew Terry felt fortunate. I know I did.

When my wife, Betsy, and I arrived in Los Angeles thirty-four years ago, after Lionel, who was then president of the temple, decided to roll the dice on a twenty-six-year-old kid from the Midwest, we were invited to dinner at Lionel and Terry's. We were fresh off the farm, and we walked into that elegant, warm, beautiful home. A Chagall painting to the left—so deeply blue and dark and beautiful—and the most amazing aromas wafting from the kitchen. We were nervous. Enter Terry, smiling warmly—not a phony or privileged bone in her body. There was talk of art, of business, and gentle, kind questions for the new rabbi barely older than a boy and his shy, sweet, equally young wife.

In some ways Terry was a beautiful contradiction. She was elegant but told the best dirty jokes. She had incredible grace and style, but had no problem mowing the lawn while pregnant. She was a great community leader, but she never upstaged Lionel and remained in some ways the sort of old-fashioned wife whose mission was to take care of her husband. They were beautiful together, laughing, teasing, traveling the world, enthralled with music, art, food, and fun. When times were good, they had a life of laughter and love, respect and team-work. When times were bad, they had a life of laughter and love, respect and teamwork. They started out in a studio apartment, sleeping on a Murphy bed. You could lie in bed and turn the kitchen faucet on with one hand and flush the toilet in the bathroom with the other. And from there they lived a remarkable life tucked beneath the covers of nearly seventy years. I still laugh when I remember Terry telling me about an upcoming trip she and Lionel were going on to tour the greatest museums and restaurants in Europe. "It sounds amazing," I responded.

"It will be a great ski vacation," she said. I was confused. I couldn't figure out what museums and restaurants in Europe had to do with skiing.

"Ski vacation?" I asked.

"Yeah, S-K-I. Spending the Kids' Inheritance!" she countered.

Three years after Terry died, I sat down with Lionel at his home for the visit he requested, and the reason for it became clear pretty quickly.

"Terry and I had a hell of a life," he told me. "We really had a good time."

"I know you miss her, Lionel. I know . . ."

"Steve, I want you to know I have decided to stop my dialysis. You know what that means?"

"I do." I knew that dialysis three days a week meant he no longer had a single day when he felt well and wasn't exhausted, but that stopping meant certain death within two weeks or less.

"And I want you to know that I feel happy about it. I feel relieved. My kids are okay with this. They have their own lives and I have done everything I can for them already. They love me, but they don't need me. I'm done. You and I have had a lot of good meals together, a lot of good scotch. You've done a hell of a job at the temple, and I love you, Steve. I've never said that to another man. Now, say goodbye to me, keep up the good work, and enjoy your life with Betsy and the kids."

We hugged. I turned toward the door, then turned back around for a smile and a wave. I blew Lionel a kiss and turned away again—deeply moved and quiet, but not in sadness. He missed Terry so much. My mind flashed to the ancient words of the Song of Solomon, "Love is as strong as death." Lionel's love for Terry and his wise understanding that more is not always better led him to a place of great peace. It was time.

How could anyone want to die? we wonder. But we wonder only because we are not actually dying. Dying makes perfect sense to the dying, just not to the living; the same way that breathing underwater makes perfect sense to the fish but not to us. But by the dying, I mean those who are minutes, hours, or days from death. I do not mean you or me. For the living, death is often a frightening, sad, mysterious stalker in our lives. When someone is really, truly dying, there is no fear, only peace. Why? Because there are many things worse than dying. Yes, some people die suddenly and tragically, but most people, even young people who die, do so at the end of a long journey through disease, the falling apart and the preparation it brings.

Whoever wrote the third chapter of Ecclesiastes (later made famous by the Byrds) was right. There really is a time for everything. Most people are ready for death the way we are all ready for sleep after a long and exhausting day. We just want to pull the covers up around our aching heads and settle in for the peace of it all. We are not anxious about sleeping. We are not depressed about it. We are not afraid of it. Disease, age, and life itself prepare us for death. There is a time for everything, and when it is our time to die, death is as natural a thing as life itself. Consider this very good news for those of us who fear death. Dying people are not afraid of dying. If you are afraid of dying, it is not your day. Anxiety is for the living. So if you are worried and anxious about dying, you're not dying. Which means you have time to let death teach you about living and loving your life.

When the greatest of all sages, Moses, dies in the Bible, it says he died "at the mouth of the Lord." This is often understood to mean Moses died with a kiss from God. Whether we are believers or not, there is mystical power in this idea that we are filled with breath when we are born, and when we die, that last, final breath is a sort of kiss—tender, loving, and kind. It is right, it is peaceful, it is everything, and it is—nothing.

In retrospect, Alzheimer's did not distance me from my dad. He grew quieter, but I grew closer, learning how much it meant just to hold his hand in perfect silence until he fell asleep. Like the sea, like the rising and setting of the sun, disease, age, and decline have their own rhythm, an internal wisdom and power that sweeps us up, carries us, schools us, enlightens us, exhausts us, and without our fully knowing it, prepares us for death, the perfect peace.

2

Showing Up

Courage starts with showing up
and letting ourselves be seen.
——BRENÉ BROWN

Although the dying usually have no worries for themselves, that is not to say that they have no worries at all. Their worries are for us, the living whom they love and will leave behind. Julie's husband, Ed, had cancer twice, two stem cell replacement therapies, and many days when no one thought he would survive. But he did. Then just a few years later, Julie was the one with cells gone mad, and they turned out to be lethal. She took her colon cancer in stride as much as anyone could. Embracing the absurdity of it all, she held "Champagne and Shitting" parties for her friends. They sat in her bedroom, drank champagne, laughed, and kept a tally of every time Julie had to run to the bathroom, which she had to do a lot as a result of the cancer and treatment. But after three years of debilitating chemo and experimental drugs, she made the decision to stop. She did not want more pain, more medicine, more anything. She wanted peace.

"I'm not afraid to die" was the first thing she told me as I sat next to her bed, looking into her still-beautiful blue eyes. Her terribly frail body was thin and wasted.

"When it's really time, no one ever is," I answered.

"Really?" She smiled. "I'm glad."

Julie wasn't afraid for herself because she knew better than most that she had no unfinished business. Her kids knew how completely she loved them. Her husband knew how they had supported each other along the way through his cancer and hers. Her friends knew how deeply she loved them and they her, as she invited them to sit on her bed while handing a piece of her jewelry to each with a wish. Julie was relieved— released from having to fight, to go on, to endure treatment after treatment, to pretend everything was going to be all right. Still, there were things she needed to hear again and again, and things she didn't need to hear.

That is why, when I met with her family, whom I've known for thirty years, to talk about where they were and where they were going on this road to death, I shared with them the most important things I have learned over these years for the family of the dying, the crucial ways of being during those final days.

Do Not Waste the Rest of Your Loved One's Life Worrying About His or Her Death

Yes, you need to be sure you have purchased a cemetery plot or cremation services and have chosen a mortuary. But once those basic decisions are made, stop. Treat the person you love like the fully alive, fully human, fully beautiful person he or she is. Enjoy him or her for every good moment of every hour of every day. Assume your loved one can hear absolutely everything you are saying in his or her presence. She is alive, treat her that way. He is alive, treat him that way.

This is another way of saying, stay in the moment as much and as often as possible. When we are under stress or face uncertainty, we all catastrophize the future to some degree. We imagine how sad we will be at the funeral. We think about how much we will miss this person. We wonder if we will ever feel joy again. The same questions run over and over through our heads: *How will I live without her? How will I feel safe without him? Will the kids be all right? Will I? What about the house? What about the money? What if something happens to me?* These are normal worries, but they are not productive.

They sap your spiritual, physical, and emotional energy when you need it most. They distance you and distract you, taking you away from your loved one and shortening the time you have left together.

When you find yourself catastrophizing about the future, stop! Remind yourself that the nightmares you are imagining are not real. The future, good or bad, never pans out the way we imagine it will in the present. Replace those frightening questions you are ruminating over with a much better set of questions. Ask yourself what you can do in the next hour that is actually meaningful for you and your loved one. What can you do that will be productive, comforting, funny, loving, and kind for you or your loved one? Keep yourself on a short time leash. Every time you start imagining the worst possible outcome of the future, pull yourself back into the present. That is where you are needed.

Travel Back with Your Loved One

One of the things that I have found to be most helpful and meaningful when a loved one is dying is to take him or her on a sort of mental vacation. The person might be bedridden, but his or her mind is free to revisit happier times. "When was your first kiss?" you might ask. "Who was she? Do you know where she is now? What was the greatest vacation you ever took? Do you remember the first time you ever laid eyes on Mom? What went through your mind? Best meal you ever ate? Funniest thing you ever did? Take me back . . ." It is amazing to watch how memories lift people above their current sorrow into the transcendent meaning embedded in reminiscing. These conversations, these moments are precious gifts unwrapped by the power and the beauty of memory.

I will always remember when, after I took a terminally ill woman down this path of memory with her husband and daughter by her bedside, her husband turned to her and said, "That was the most beautiful hour we have spent together in months." What I think he meant was that the memories were a reminder of a greater whole that could and should define their lives, more so than the disease she was succumbing to.

One of the crueler aspects of my father's disease was that he slowly forgot not only his past but also how to swallow. This would sometimes cause him to aspirate food into his lungs and then contract pneumonia, which could have been deadly. The only way to mitigate that cruel condition was to put him on a diet of pureed food and liquid thickened with a dissolving powder. Picture a grown man wearing a bib and being fed what was essentially baby food a spoonful at a time by the nursing home staff. For a guy who loved to eat as much as my dad did, this was a cruel fate. "Dad, remember the pancakes at the Town Talk?" I would prod before the days when it seemed that he no longer could access anything from his past. It was one of many places and meals I revisited with him in hopes that it would raise him above his current sorrow. "What about the mostaccioli and meatballs at Cafe di Napoli, the butter pecan ice cream at Bridgeman's, or the corned beef hash at the Lincoln Del, extra crispy? Remember, Dad?" It always made him smile.

I continued to take my dad on mental vacations even toward the end of his life when there was little chance that he could actually remember what I was talking about. The memory of that one-sided conversation helped me. Even now, when I am melancholy with grief, I think about *Blazing Saddles*. It is one of only two or three movies I can ever recall seeing with my dad. There is a scene in the film where the bad guys, who are morons, are chasing the good guys through the desert. In order to slow the idiot bad guys down, the good guys set up a fake tollbooth in the middle of the desert, knowing their pursuers will be too stupid to just ride their horses around the gate and stay in hot pursuit. The good guys are right. Instead of riding around the tollbooth, the villains all wait in line behind the gate while one of them yells, "Somebody's gotta go back and get a shitload of dimes." After someone finally arrives with the dimes, they stay in line and each wait their turn, putting in their dime and waiting for the tollbooth arm to lift before riding through it. For whatever reason, my dad laughed at that scene like I had never heard him laugh before. There were tears streaming down his face at the ludicrousness of it all. I love that memory of him. It lifted me from my sadness when his disease was all that I could see, and it still does.

The Soviet psychologist Bluma Zeigarnik proved that when you show people a picture of a circle with a small wedge cut out of it, their eyes first go to the missing piece every time. It is easy, among the doctors, the needles and the tubes, to lose sight of the beauty that was. Despite our pain, our fear, and our very real losses, we would do well to think about our many past blessings with our loved one who is now diminished. There is so much more to who we were and who we are than just the missing piece.

Go for the Laugh if You Possibly Can

Yes, death is sad, serious, and heavy. But life is not always thus. Death is an opportunity to reaffirm the blessing of life. Laughter is a reminder that the world will somehow go on and that our hearts will heal. When I am with mourners at their home following a funeral and out of the corner of my eye and within earshot I see and hear them laughing about some

funny thing their loved one said or did, I know they will survive their grief. To laugh is to choose to survive, to heal, and
to live.

So when I visit with a dying person, assuming the circumstances are right, I often share a funny memory I have of her
or him; something we experienced together or a funny story I
know about them. Sometimes I ask if he or she wants to hear
my new favorite joke. I warn them that the joke is just a little
off-color. They almost always say yes, and they always laugh;
that laughter is a brief escape for the dying and a reminder to
the living that life really does go on.

In case you are one of those people who has trouble remembering or telling jokes, here is one of my new favorites.

Three elderly women are sitting by the pool at their as-
sisted living residence. One of them notices an elderly man
napping on a lounge chair, flat on his back and totally naked
except for a towel over his face and another over his privates.
"Who's that?" one woman asks her two friends.

"I don't know," one of them answers. "Let's go find out."

They walk over to the sleeping man. One of the women
gently lifts the towel from his waist, takes a look, replaces the
towel, and says, "It's not my husband."

The second woman also gingerly lifts the towel, examines
the naked man, puts the towel back in place, and says, "It's not
my husband, either."

Finally the third woman lifts the towel from the man's waist, takes a long, careful look, puts the towel back, shrugs, and says, "He doesn't even live in the complex!"

And just for good measure, here's another one, about two elderly women sitting in church at the Sunday service. It's hot in the sanctuary and the pastor is droning on and on. Finally one woman turns and whispers to her friend, "This service is so long and the pastor is so boring, my behind is asleep." To which the friend replies, "I know. I already heard it snore twice."

You see, laughter really is a gift. Allow the dying to enjoy that gift and you will be giving yourself hope while you do.

Give an Academy Award–Winning Performance Despite Your Fears

I said earlier that people do not fear for themselves when they are dying, but that does not mean they have no fears. The fears that dying people express to me at the end of their lives are fears about whether or not the people they love will be okay. We are never worried about ourselves when we are dying, we just want to be sure our spouse, children, grandchildren, brothers, sisters, parents, or dearest friends are going to be happy again and well. This means that despite the very real concerns we might have for ourselves as we face the death of a loved one, these are not fears to be shared with the dying. That's where the Academy Award part comes in.

Even if you have to pretend a little or a lot, you need to tell that person you love who is dying that you will be okay. Say things like "You did a great job and we are all going to be fine. We are going to take care of Mom. We are going to take care of Dad. I will take great care of the kids. The kids will take great care of me. You do not have to worry about us." Whichever way you put it, the message is, you won. You succeeded. You leave no unfinished emotional business with us. "We love you. We will take care of one another. You can rest. You can let go because you have taught us and given us everything we need to be okay when you are gone."

This is what I was getting at when during that conversation in the nursing home when Dad could still nod yes or no, I told him that the work ethic he gave me made me successful. I told him that no matter what, I would be able to take care of myself and my family when he was gone. I know that making me self-sufficient and successful was the reason he made me work so hard as a child. Did he overdo it? Yes. Did I suffer from missing out on the fun that most other kids had with their dads? Yes. Have I paid an emotional and physical price for my workaholism bequeathed to me by my dad? Yes. Did I say any of that to my dad during what I believed was my last conversation with him when he could still understand who I was and what I was saying? No. These goodbye conversations are not therapy for the living, but a gift for the dying, a peace offering from those of us who will be left behind.

I have been witness to the power of permission to die countless times. So often, after I gather with a family to hold hands around the bedside of their dying loved one as each shares a blessing for that person and gives him or her permission to let go, within hours, death arrives as a sort of peaceful friend. It is permission granted, and in that moment, we are like a soft breeze—quiet, barely there, then . . . gone.

Don't Underestimate the Power
of Simply Being with Someone

My father's inability to speak and to remember taught me new lessons about the importance of touch. When nothing else would pierce the depths of his dying brain, a world that he seemed to inhabit entirely alone, I would give him a scalp massage or a shoulder rub. It made his face light up every time, bringing him back from the depths. In a way, that touching amid the silence assured my dad that I was there and that he too was somehow there. We were there together. I never imagined that I would be comfortable in the quiet, just holding my dad's hand. I was moved by the soundless power of it all; saying so much by way of the unspoken.

I think touch is what people missed most during the 2020 pandemic, especially people quarantined alone. Touch is the most necessary and beautiful of all the senses, a wordless language of love. It gave my father and me a connection in some ways more intimate and real than any we had ever had before.

After more than three decades of standing in hospital hallways and on the front steps of the dying, I still am never sure of what I am going to say when I cross the threshold and our eyes meet. I never know for certain because I never know how close to dying the person I am visiting is or what state of mind he or she will be in. I tell myself the same thing I tell everyone who calls me for advice before visiting a loved one whose days are few: Don't worry about what to say, just walk in the door and the rest will unfold. Just show up. Through years of experience and hundreds of walked-through doors, I know that when we are openhearted and present, something beautiful will emerge.

My friend David has been chronicling each day of his life since everything changed, when he was diagnosed with cancer. One of his most moving observations is about vulnerability and the beauty of showing up.

Sister Anne is with us. She flew in from San Diego last night. This is news, because she has not flown since 9/11; the flight went smoothly, and we have been catching up on all manner of things. She will now have the pleasure of accompanying us to doctor's appointments, and we will do some surveying of the vast rebuilding going on around Santa Rosa in the wake of the fires of almost two years ago.

Aging and humility. At some point in one's life, if you live long enough, you pretty much have to think about getting old. For me this has been particularly troublesome because I have enjoyed excellent health most of the way. Some years ago, Ruth and I attended a lecture by a superb gerontologist. He described old age as a declining sawtooth curve; one's health declines in periodic illnesses, from which we recover, but not back to the level previous to the illness.

Everybody is different. In my case, the diagnosis of acute myeloid leukemia marked an undeniable moment. I am no longer on a sagging continuum. Though I feel little different from before the diagnosis, a lot became different on April 25 from what it was on April 24. Daily life is significantly about staying alive. Much time is spent on this, and my physical abilities took a dive from which there is not likely to be much of a recovery.

And this is where the humility has to come in. The priorities have to change. Particular uncertainties are now magnified. Certain preparations are now in order. Essentially, I am simply not in control of as much as I am accustomed to or would like.

Given all of this, one realizes a profound connection and even dependency that may have been there but went largely unnoticed: relations with friends and family. "Profound" is too weak a word. When Sister Anne finally, reluctantly, gets on an airplane and makes her way to Santa Rosa, she makes a statement. All of you have, for which I thank you.

When I last saw Franny, she was in her at-home hospital bed set up in the middle of the den, the hub of the house, where much of her family's life had been lived, sheltered, nurtured, and enjoyed. She was bloated and exhausted from a five-year war with cancer that was now coming to an end. Our eyes met, and she just opened her arms wide to me with a smile. "Can I hug you?" I asked.

"Yes, please," she answered.

I leaned over the bed and said nothing. We just hugged as Franny sighed and wept. What mattered in that moment was not what I said, but simply that I was there. The hug lasted a long time, reminding me yet again how important touch can be, and then came the words.

"What are you thinking about?" I asked.

"The kids," she said.

"Well, catch me up. What's happening with them?" As I

hear about Chloe and Bobby, Franny's face lights up. She is a proud mom. We laugh about their naiveté, their ambition, their millennial foolishness. Franny is dying, but she is Franny and I am me.

Be your most authentic self as you spend the last few days or speak the last few words with the person who is dying. This is no time to be something new or different. Do not try to forge a new persona in the face of death, just be you. If you are a hugger, hug. If you are a feeder, feed. If you are a joker, joke. If you are a gossip, dish away. Be with someone in death as you were in life. That is what the mourners and what a person who is dying wants and needs the most. Sit with them at home or in the hospital lounge and just be who you have always been. They want and need some normalcy, some comfort of the familiar; they need you, the authentic, real you. When people call me worried about what to say or how to be around the dying or their loved ones, they are surprised when I tell them, "You already know how to be, so there is nothing to prepare for. Just walk in the door and be yourself."

Of course, when the authentic you happens to be a rabbi, the conversations and questions are in some ways different from most. Sometimes people who are dying share their dreams with me. Our dreams often change as we near death. They become more about people who have already died and less about the living. They become more vivid. This is true when we are not dreaming too. The dying often tell me that sounds and colors become more vibrant—the red redder, the green greener, the music sweeter and more beautiful.

"My mother died when I was only eight," Franny tells me. "I am dreaming about her a lot now. I am in the passenger seat of a car and someone I cannot see is driving me, but I somehow know that it is my mother. She is taking me on a journey, but I don't know where. I just know it is with her and I feel peaceful."

I go with this, not against it. "That's beautiful," I say. "The idea of your mother whom you missed so much in life waiting for you in death is really beautiful."

"It is," Franny says. And then she asks, "Is it normal to dream like that?" Whenever someone dying asks me if their feelings are normal, I always say yes. Our job as a friend is to go with them on their journey, not to ask them to take whatever detour we think we would take if we were them or to talk them into or out of something we deeply feel or deeply believe. This seems so obvious, but I cannot tell you how many times I have heard people try to redirect the thoughts of the dying to something that makes the living more comfortable. Showing up for someone requires the courage to go with that person wherever he or she wants to go, even if it makes us uncomfortable.

We move from Franny's dreams to her fears. When some-one is actively dying, within a few days of his or her last breath, I always ask a simple three-word question at their bed-side: "Are you afraid?" I have asked that simple question for well over three decades, and the answer has always been no. Franny's only fear is that the people she loves will need her and are going to suffer the pain of her loss forever. That fear is very real; there is no denying it. We sit with it for a moment. Speaking of a fear is an important way to manage it. Then I remind Franny that nearly every child, including Franny her-self, survives a parent's death somehow.

Even when the reverse occurs, the most unnatural of deaths—that of a parent outliving a child—life reasserts itself. I have helped parents bury children in a coffin the size of a shoebox, and five or ten years later I bump into those same parents at the movies and see them laughing and eating pop-corn. Not because they have forgotten their sorrow, not be-cause they do not ache sometimes, and not because they are exceptional, but because they are human, like all of us, with a capacity to move forward in life despite the worst pain of death and grief.

"Your children will be sad," I tell Franny, "but they will not die because you die. They will live and laugh and love with everything you have given them in their hearts forever. They will discover you in unexpected moments and places for the rest of their lives. My dad died two years ago now, Franny, and I promise you, he is not gone. I discover him in new and beautiful ways all the time. I can hear his voice telling me what to do, making me laugh; he's with me still.

"What would you like me to say at the funeral? What should I tell people? What do you want them to know?" Whenever it is possible, I ask people these questions because I want them to have the final word about their own funeral. And those final words are usually both terse and perfect—the distillate of an entire life. These sorts of questions are a part of being fearless with those who are dying. This is what it really means to show up. You can ask these sorts of questions even if you are not going to formally eulogize them at their funeral. Ask so that you can share the answers for the rest of your life with their children, their siblings, and their friends, and you can store them within your own heart when they are gone.

"I want people to laugh and find the fun in life. Tell them to remember my life, not my death," Franny answered.

"Perfect, Franny. Perfect. What else would you like?"

We talk about the music she wanted played at her funeral, because music is important to her and she has given the subject a lot of thought. She asks me to listen to a couple of songs with her to help narrow it down to two for the funeral. She decides she wants to open with the adagio from Mozart's

Clarinet Concerto and close with Warren Zevon's "Keep Me in Your Heart." "I like it, Franny. Just like you—highbrow and a rocker all in one." We laugh. Then we listen to "Keep Me in Your Heart" one more time.

It is time to say goodbye. After two hours Franny is exhausted, and I have more appointments to keep. Somehow the mundane reasserts itself with both the living and the dying. I point this out to Franny when she tells me about the lineup of friends who have been by the past few days to visit and say goodbye. There is no pretending they will see Franny alive again—and yet there is a strange normalcy to each visit, because the truth is that dying is both strange and normal at the same time.

"Saying goodbye is not all that dramatic, is it?" I ask, already knowing the answer. I have said goodbye to so many dying people with a hug, a kiss, or a gentle wave, and then I turn and walk out the door—amazed by the ordinariness of it all. Perhaps it is because the dying are ready to die and the living somehow know it. There is a sort of inevitability to parting; life is full of endings. But whatever the reason, and despite Hollywood's creations to the contrary, I affirm for Franny that saying goodbye, while poignant and sweet, is also mostly ordinary.

"So let's have our mundane goodbye now, Franny."

"Okay." She gives a little laugh.

The visit ends as it began, with a hug. I am bent over her hospital bed. We are cheek to cheek, and she whispers, "I wish you so much love."

"And I wish you perfect peace, my friend, and everlasting love. May perfect peace be yours soon." I turn and walk out the door. I do not look back.

I am in my car in Franny's driveway, my thumbs flying across the keyboard of my phone, jotting down notes from our conversation. Later, when I arrive home, I go in my study to clean up and impose some order on my notes so they are well organized for later, when it's time to write Franny's eulogy. Graham Greene famously said that there is a "splinter of ice in the heart of a writer" which allows him or her to take notes in the midst of tragedy. This is true of me in the midst of death and in the midst of life. I am always searching for the sermon. It is how I find and reveal meaning in the aftermath of seeing and feeling so much: leaving someone's deathbed; standing with a young couple beneath the wedding canopy; naming a newborn baby; watching my wife sleep as the early morning light slowly differentiates her from the receding shadows of night, noticing as if for the first time her smooth skin and tousled hair.

Through most of my day, nearly every day, I am taking notes for later, for some future listener or reader, and for me. As I stared into my father's casket, wondering if they had made some sort of terrible mistake because he did not look exactly like himself, I was in the surreal fog of death that both dulls and heightens our senses. I was there, but I was also observing myself observing, storing the image, the feeling—for later, when I can make some sense of it all. What kind of person takes notes for later while standing in front of his father's open casket? Albert Einstein supposedly said, "There are only two ways to live your life. One is as though nothing is a miracle. The other is as though everything is a miracle." Never do I feel the miracle of life more so than in the face of death.

I do not know that any of us could go on without seeking and finding some order, some meaning and purpose to life. Sometimes I wonder, as all thinking people do, if life is ultimately meaningless and it is we who imbue it with invented purpose. But being so proximate to so many as their physical lives come to an end, I do not think so—mostly because of how much it hurts us when someone we love is gone. That pain is the surest sign to me that life matters. That Franny matters. My notes are not imposing meaning, they are revealing it.

At home, I Google the lyrics to Warren Zevon's "Keep Me in Your Heart" because I am sad and want to listen to it again. Occasionally I just want to feel fully present, with no obligation to articulate those feelings to others as if they were theirs. It takes an act of will for me to melt that splinter of ice, to bridge the distance between me and my deeper feelings so that I feel more keenly the sadness and the suffering of my own heart, both bruised and made more beautiful by saying goodbye to so many.

When I am sick of death, I drink scotch sometimes. I want to be numb. Other times I come home and fall into my wife's arms. I do not want to talk; I want to be held, I want to be fully human, I want to care, to really embrace and really learn and really face the truth of death. I listen to the song in order to thaw, to release, to feel. Rabbi Leder had done his job. Steve Leder needed to cry.

After I listen to the song a few times, teary-eyed, I travel down the Warren Zevon Google rabbit hole. First I search images, then Wikipedia, and then a dozen or so YouTube videos. One moves me deeply. It was Zevon's last appearance on *The David Letterman Show*. Letterman was, as Zevon himself said, "my music's greatest friend." Letterman gave Zevon great airtime over twenty years and was clearly in awe of his humor and talent as a songwriter. This particular interview would be the last time Zevon was a guest on Letterman's show and they both knew it. I continue to marvel at Letterman's extraordinary courage and skill in conducting the interview. He was rabbi-like in his fearless, gentle candor.

Letterman: I guess a couple of months ago we all learned that your life has changed radically, hasn't it?

Zevon: You mean you heard about the flu?

Letterman: Well yes, kind of about the flu.

Zevon: Well, it's true.

Letterman: How did you learn about it and how have things been since?

Zevon: Well, first of all, let me say that I might have made a tactical error in not going to a physician for twenty years . . . it was one of those phobias that really didn't pay off. The only person that I ever go to is Dr. Stan, you know, Dr. Stan the dentist. I always said if he can't fix it, I'm screwed! I told Dr. Stan that I was having shortness of breath. When Dr. Stan heard about it, he said, "It sounds like congestive heart failure."

Letterman: And it turned out not to be congestive heart failure?

Zevon: No, it's a lung cancer that's spread.

Letterman: That's tough.

Zevon: Well, it means you better get your dry cleaning done on special. . . .

Letterman: You have spent a lot of time recently working very hard, haven't you—working on another project?

Zevon: Yeah, they certainly don't discourage you from doing whatever you want. It's not like bed rest and a lot of water will straighten you out.

Letterman: And how is that work now under this circumstance, living with this diagnosis? How is the work now [compared to] when you assumed you were healthy?

Zevon: I'm working harder. You put more value on every minute. I always thought I kind of did that. I really always enjoyed myself, but it's more valuable now. You're reminded to enjoy every sandwich and every minute playing with the guys and being with the kids and everything.

Letterman: I'm stricken now, and I guess this is the way things like this work, by the irony of your work now—when we look at it and knowing about the diagnosis.

Zevon: That's the strangest part to me, certainly.

Letterman: For example, the title of the new CD, *My Ride's Here*. That has a whole different meaning. And another song, the one Paul played, "I'll Sleep When I'm Dead," and the previous album is called *Life'll Kill Ya*.

Zevon: I guess artists have some kind of instincts or, you know, feelings about things that can't be put into words; you know, kind of impressions combined with very rudimentary manual skills. Otherwise how would you get away with having a job so easy and so much fun?

Letterman: So you're saying that you think maybe somewhere this comes as not so much a surprise to you.

Zevon: I did take the copies of the albums to my doctors and say, "This is why I'm not so shocked." I don't know what the connection is. I don't know why I was writing those songs. But you know, I've always written those songs.

Letterman: From your perspective now, do you know something about life and death that maybe I don't know now?

This was Letterman's equivalent to my question for Franny and for my dad and so many others. It was his "Are you afraid?" and his "What would you like me to say to everyone who will be at the funeral?" These sorts of questions almost always elicit, in the simplest terms, the wisdom of a lifetime perfectly revealed by impending death. Zevon's answer? "I know how much you're supposed to enjoy every sandwich."

"After the show, it was heartbreaking," Letterman told *Rolling Stone* in 2008 about that last interview with Zevon.

"We were talking and this and that. Here's a guy who had months to live and we're making small talk. And as we're talking, he's taking his guitar strap and hooking it, wrapping it around. Then he puts the guitar into the case and he flips the snaps on the case and says, 'Here, I want you to have this, take good care of it.' And I just started sobbing. He was giving me the guitar that he always used on the show. I felt like, 'I can't be in this movie, I didn't get my lines.' That was very tough."

I don't know why Warren Zevon gave that guitar to David Letterman, but if I had to guess, it was to thank him for giving his music so much attention over the years, creating a larger and more lasting legacy for the beauty, the humor, the irony, and the poignancy of his art. I know Zevon brought that to Franny and to everyone who wept at her funeral while his music played. And I'd guess it was a thank-you for that interview—for the fearless way Letterman showed up, even in front of millions of viewers, and allowed Zevon to talk openly and truthfully, expressing the essentialism that only death creates. It was for the way that, in showing up, Letterman helped Zevon distill the lesson of his death and therefore his life into a simple, beautiful imperative: "Enjoy every sandwich."

A few days after I watched the Letterman interview, an email arrives from Franny's husband: "Dear Rabbi, After a five-year courageous battle, Franny died last night surrounded by her family. Now what?"

3

In Death as in Life

Life and death.
They are somehow sweetly and beautifully mixed,
but I don't know how.
—GLORIA SWANSON

I keep a red ceramic bowl on the coffee table in my office. The table is in front of what I call my couch of tears—the place where people sit when they come to me brokenhearted from a loss of some kind. Maybe it's the loss of their marriage or their reputation or their health. Often they are there to talk about loss because of a loved one's impending death. What should they say? What should they do? How can they make things better? The bowl serves two purposes. The first is to collect the tear-soaked tissues that are an inevitable part of so many conversations that take place on that couch. Tears accompany loss.

The second purpose that red bowl serves is to help me answer the "How can I make things better?" question. "Better?" I usually ask. "What do you hope gets better?" And then the painful truths tumble out. Accounts of family dysfunction, petty jealousies, gossip, sniping, decades of tension or neglect; stories of fathers and sons, mothers and daughters, brothers and sisters who rarely if ever speak. An impending death comes with a certain amount of fantastical thinking for most people. I do not mean the kind of hope we hold on to medically—hope that the next clinical trial drug works or an organ donor materializes before it is too late. The kind of hope I am talking about involves the sudden healing of a dysfunctional family or relationship simply because someone is dying.

So often people come to me and more or less express this wish, this hope, this fantasy—that because someone is dying, their relationship with that person will improve. Experience has taught me this is rarely the case. So many times, I point to that bowl and ask, "Do you see that bowl? You can stare at that bowl all day long, all week long, all month long, all year long, and it will not change. You can go to therapy with that bowl, you can speak to that bowl and ask it firmly, nicely, calmly, or angrily to become a spoon, but that bowl will never become a spoon no matter what you say or do. And the longer you plead with that bowl to change, the more you, not the bowl, become the fool."

One of my favorite old jokes goes like this:

Ralph is on his deathbed and his brother Charlie is hovering over him.

"Charlie, I have a terrible confession to make," Ralph says weakly. "I want to repent for my sins. I am truly, truly sorry."

"What could you have done that was so bad?" Charlie asks.

"Remember when someone robbed our company of two hundred and fifty thousand dollars while you were on vacation? I took the money."

"That's all right," soothes Charlie. "This is no time to think of things like that."

"And when you created that new pattern that would have put us ahead of every other garment maker in the country, I stole the drawings and sold them to our competitor before our own company could get it on the market."

"Shh, shh. Try to rest," croons Charlie.

"And Charlie, I was the one who convinced your wife to leave you so that I could marry her and get even more of your money."

Ralph is now sobbing with remorse. "Oh, Charlie, please forgive me before I die!"

"What's to forgive?" Charlie answers. "We're even. I'm the one who poisoned you!"

Seriously, most often, troubled relationships and troubled people stay that way, even in the face of death.

As a boy, I tagged along to work with my father at the junkyard he owned with my uncle Mort. The work they did was hard physical labor. Dad and Uncle Mort had started out poor, picking tin cans out of the garbage at the dump, taking them to the local scrapyard, and pocketing a few bucks.

Next they bought an old truck and started servicing accounts. They didn't even have a building at first. A friend let them park the truck in his coal yard. They worked outside, suffering from frostbite in the Minnesota cold. With no place to lock up their tools at night, they hid them by piling coal on top of them and then dug them out each morning.

Dad and Uncle Mort took the jobs no one else wanted: pulling cast-iron boilers, brass fittings, and copper pipes out of burned-out, dangerous condemned buildings. At some point they bought a little piece of land and put up a shed to stay warm. They bought more trucks and serviced more accounts. They managed to buy a double lot in the suburbs and built two houses on it; the two of them raised, clothed, fed, and educated all their children.

After twenty years Dad and Uncle Mort had made it. But

the more they made, the further they seemed to drift apart. These two brothers needed each other, but I don't think they actually loved each other—some past history involving their parents favoring one over the other poisoned the well long, long ago. Eventually they became next-door neighbors whose wives lost touch and whose children barely interacted. I worked at the junkyard every Saturday when I was a kid. I remember listening to them argue about who did what for whom, about who was lazy, who really made the money, who really screwed up the deals gone bad, and where the stapler belonged on the desk.

My dad and his brother were locked in a sort of Greek tragedy for most of their lives. During the second-to-last act, when my father's Alzheimer's had progressed to the point that he could no longer work, my family had to enter into arbitration with Mort in order to fight for what was rightfully my father's. When the day arrived for the hearing, the sign on the law firm's conference room door read *Leder v. Leder*. It was one of the saddest moments of my life. Sadder still was the fact that for the final four decades of their lives, these brothers were in a last-to-die competition with each other. Instead of splitting up their business and parting ways in peace, each was waiting for the other to die so that the last man standing could declare victory. Mort actually died a couple of years before my father, so in a sense, despite how twisted it sounds,

Dad won—triumphing over the older brother he had suffered at the hand of for much of his life. But by the time he had won this terrible race to the bottom, Dad's Alzheimer's was so severe he had no idea who Mort was or that Mort had even died. It was a tragic conclusion and a terrible waste. When I was younger, I used to think that it was always possible to make things better between people. But that isn't true. There wasn't anything any of us could do to repair what was broken between Dad and Mort, and the fact that they were both old and dying changed . . . nothing.

"Rabbi, my father and I have had a pretty rocky relationship most of my life, but now that he has been diagnosed with pancreatic cancer and has only a few months, I am sure we are going to become closer than ever before," a young man seated on my couch of tears says to me.

"I doubt it," I regrettably have to answer. "If I were you, I would not set myself up for that kind of likely disappointment. In my experience, dying does not give someone a new personality. If you had problems with your father during his life, you are likely going to have those same problems with him during his death. In fact, maybe more so. It is sort of like the quote attributed to the German poet Heinrich Heine: 'The Jews are like everyone else, just more so.'" Death does not change the essential nature of a person or a family, it just makes everything and everyone more so. Yes, there are rare exceptions, but generally speaking, families who are dysfunctional in life are dysfunctional in death. Loving, close families in life are loving, close families in death.

That young man and his father diagnosed with pancreatic cancer are not likely to have an idyllic relationship during the last few months of the father's life. It might seem like the wrong thing to tell him, but in my view, this is exactly what he needs to hear. Why? Because making peace with death is really about making peace with life—accepting the things that cannot be changed so that we do not exhaust ourselves, fool ourselves, or consider ourselves failures if we are not able to fundamentally alter the nature of another person. There was no fixing his dad in life, so there will be no fixing his dad in death. Accepting this truth releases the son from blaming himself and keeps him from trying to do something futile.

Alzheimer's robbed my father of many things, but he also remained essentially the same—tough. When I was a kid, my uncle Mort and my cousin Mark had an old, fire-engine-red Ford Model A truck they had restored and kept in their garage. When Mort used to drive us around the neighborhood in it, I felt like the grand master of a parade. One day when I was maybe five or six years old, Mark was working on the truck in the garage, and for some reason my dad and I were there. Suddenly the truck's engine caught on fire. The black smoke of burning insulation and rubber was everywhere, and there were flames creeping out from underneath the hood. I watched my dad lift the hood, reach right into the middle of the flames, and start pulling wires out with his bare hands to see if he could stop the fire. The wires burned through the flesh of my dad's palms almost to the bone. He didn't scream. He didn't panic. Instead, he wrapped his hands in his T-shirt, walked me home, and calmly asked my mother to drive him to the ER. A normal person would have writhed and screamed. My dad was silent in his pain.

It was true then, and it was true during the ten years he suffered with Alzheimer's. Ten years of a catheter and urinary tract infections. Ten years of aspirating food and subsequent pneumonias. Bedsores. A terrible rash on his penis, groin, and butt. Ten years of having to be fed, diapered, and bathed like a baby. Ten fucking years. My dad's capacity to withstand pain amazed me as a child, and the sight and the smell of those lines of burnt flesh on his palms are seared in my memory. My memories of him in that nursing home are no less searing. My dad's capacity to take it, to withstand his suffering during the last ten years of his life, amazed me as a grown-up no less than he amazed that little boy in the garage. He faced that slow, decade-long death and all of its horrible indignities the same way he faced the painful indignities of his life—a mostly terrible marriage, a half century of aggravation with his brother, and plenty more—with a mighty and powerful silence. This is the beauty and the tragedy of my father's life and death. For him, for me, for most of us most of the time, for better and for worse, death is life's mirror.

Over the years I have buried a lot of people whose deaths left their family and friends with terrible feelings of guilt. This is particularly true of suicides and overdoses. When these feelings are expressed to me and I respond with the simple truth that most people die the way they live, it actually helps the family and diminishes their guilt. If no matter how hard they tried, they could do little to affect the severity of their loved one's mental illness or addiction, then their loved one's death can hardly be their fault. Some deaths are inevitable because people die the way they live.

Sometimes it is the dying person who wants to make a dramatic change at the end of his or her life. My friend Paul had three different types of cancer, the third of which was fatal. He came to see me during the last few months of his life. Paul told me that his energy was waning, and despite his promise to himself to begin a journal for his young children, he had not started anything. It was bothering Paul that he wasn't chronicling his thoughts each day so that his daughters would have them years later. He knew I was a writer and he wanted some advice about how to push through writer's block. "Have you ever journaled?" I asked him.

"No," he answered. "I have never been the kind of person who records his own life or thoughts. I have always cared more about experiencing life than writing about it."

I went on to tell Paul that if he had never journaled before, he wasn't likely to do so now. Paul needed to enjoy every minute of his remaining time with his wife and daughters, not spend his final days fretting about this or trying to become a different person. Paul was relieved to have permission to be who he was in life when he was facing death instead of trying to become someone else.

I gave the same basic insight to my friend Ali, whose mother was dying fifteen years after a debilitating stroke. Before the stroke, her mother had doted on her father. They were best friends, business partners, lovers, parents, and grandparents. They had separate bodies, but they were in so many ways one soul.

For fifteen years, Ali's father, Ben, spent nearly every waking moment caring for his wife, schlepping her in the wheelchair to movies and plays; to their grandchildren's recitals, soccer games, and graduations; to family dinners, shopping, museums—you name it. He never wanted her to miss an important or even an ordinary moment. Now her body was almost completely used up, but Ben kept trying to keep her connected to life. So much so that Ali wanted him to just stop pushing her mother to do things and instead to just let her rest, let her go. She called me in frustration with her dad. "Ali, before the stroke, what was your parents' relationship like?" I asked.

"They were best friends. They did everything together. They were so devoted to each other, it was hard for other people to believe."

"Well, why would that change now?" I asked Ali.

"Because she's dying," she answered.

"Big mistake," was my response. "Ali, if your parents were fiercely devoted to each other in life, they are going to remain that way in death. There is no possible way that your father is going to stop doting on your mother, or stop trying to rally her, or stop trying to keep her connected to life until her last breath. And the only thing you are going to do by trying to change him and the way he loves your mother is to add more stress to an already stressful situation. Let him be, Ali. Let him be who he has always been for your mother."

This very simple insight, that most of us tend to face death the same way we faced life, is mind-blowing for a lot of people when they first hear it. It changes the context of death from something foreign and filled with wishful thinking to something familiar that both the living and the dying have lived and understood for many years. For Paul, for Ali, for all of us who think we can impose our will, it is usually far better to let people be how they have always been, good or bad, than try to change them or ourselves before they or we die. I do not mean to suggest that something wrong cannot ever be made right. Dying can sometimes cause people to recognize and apologize for past mistakes, and those apologies can be sincerely accepted. But such reconciliations are far rarer than most people think. So many times on that couch of tears I remind people of how important it is when facing death to ride with the current rather than fight against it. Most often, that is the path to greater peace and understanding. You cannot push a river upstream.

Here is perhaps the toughest and yet most liberating truth about the fact that people die the way they live. If you have had a hopelessly toxic relationship with someone, even someone as close as a parent or a sibling—a relationship fraught with feelings of guilt, remorse, anger, and disappointment—you do not need to try to repair it before that person dies. You simply need to accept it. And contrary to the fact that people will say things to you like "You should try to make peace before [that person] dies because you will feel guilty later if you don't," the truth is that you will not have more regret when a person who has hurt you for years or a person with whom you could just never really get along or be close to dies. You will be relieved. I know that sounds harsh, but it is the truth. A torturous relationship in life is less painful when death finally comes, and that relief is nothing to feel guilty about.

The good news is that there is often beauty in families facing death the way they faced life. Countless times I have joined the family of a dying person around his or her bedside, all of us holding hands, praying, sharing loving stories, tears, and laughter. There is no conflict in the goodbye surrounding death because there was no conflict in life that they didn't get past. A funny person in life will find humor even in death. A good example is my friend Paul, whom I relieved of guilt for not journaling his last few weeks of life. When he was just days away from dying of that third cancer, he looked up at me and said, "This much character I don't need." The comedian Rodney Dangerfield, who was definitely funny in life, is buried in a row of celebrities in a famous Los Angeles cemetery. His headstone reads: "There goes the neighborhood!" The kind of people who are open and honest with family and friends throughout their lives will be just as open and honest about death. There will be no unfinished business between them and their loved ones in death because there was none in life. The tough will be tough, the funny will be funny, the truthful will be honest, and the loving will be loving. Most people die exactly the way they live. This is sometimes terrible and sometimes beautiful, but it is almost always true.

. . .

If we really think about it rather than avoid it, most of us have an idea of our ideal death that is a reflection of our ideals in life. We have a sense of how we would like our final days to be lived and our funeral conducted. Almost all of us can actually plan for our deaths to a pretty significant degree, because most of us will die as the result of a long illness or old age, the trajectories of which can more or less be predicted. Most of us can choose to have a good death in the same way we have made plans for a good life. But plan we must.

In order to make sure you can die the way you lived, meaning in control of your own destiny and according to your own values, you must appoint someone who can speak for you if and when you can no longer speak for yourself. Choose uncompromising advocates who will never let you down. Most people say they want to die at home, but 80 percent of Americans die somewhere other than their homes. Saying you want to die at home is not the same as having a plan. Saying, "If that ever happens to me, shoot me," is not a plan.

We all should have a medical directive document in our files and given to our loved ones, doctors, and lawyers. We should also appoint at least one person, preferably two, who can speak for us when we cannot make or articulate decisions for ourselves and then write those wishes down very clearly. That way our advocates will not have to read our minds or equivocate. Instead, they can say no on our behalf to the ICU or another trip to the ER and yes to hospice and palliative care. Empower your advocates to make sure your caregivers are the right caregivers, and if they aren't, to fire them and find others, again and again and again if necessary. We went through many caregivers during my father's illness, but when we found Robert, things were so much better for my dad and for the rest of us. Despite fielding countless requests from families to thank their loved one's caregivers in my remarks at a funeral, I never fully understood the magnitude of gratitude owed the human angels and saints who care for the frail and the dying until my father was among them. Empower your designated advocate to manage your caregivers. If your loved one is being cared for by others, respect them, thank them, and honor them.

Robert learned Yiddish so that he could share a word or joke with my dad. Of course, because Robert wasn't a Jew, his Yiddish was awful. Sometimes my dad would shake his head as if to say, "Not quite, Robert." But most of the time my father smiled with delight when Robert tried to string a few Yiddish words together. Nearly every day Robert played Hank Williams and Johnny Cash, my dad's favorites, on his guitar, and he and my dad wrote songs together. He knew how much my dad loved the trees, the birds, the lakes, and the sounds of Minnesota in the summer, so Robert made sure to take Dad out in his wheelchair each sunny day, touring the nursing home's neighborhood so Dad could take it all in, in his own way.

Even the best nursing homes are filled with very vulnerable people and staff who are overworked and underpaid. It was Robert who made sure my father was clean, his teeth brushed, his nose hair trimmed, his eyeglasses sparkling, his diaper changed, his room dusted, his food pureed to reduce the risk of aspirating and dying of pneumonia. Not a weekday went by when my mother, my four siblings, and I didn't receive an email from Robert telling us how he and my dad spent their time together that day. My mother visited, pretty often at first, although the cold nature of their marriage soon reasserted itself and she appeared less and less over the years. My siblings who live in Minneapolis visited often, and so did their spouses and children. The staff at the nursing home was generally cheerful and well intentioned. But it was Robert who did the dirty work and who delighted my dad with songs and books and terrible Yiddish. Robert, more than anyone, gave my dad the best life possible, until we suddenly learned that he had been fired and could no longer take care of my dad. When the company he worked for was bought out by a larger one, for whatever reason they decided not to retain him. From that day on, my father's life was never as good. The next time I would see Robert was when he was seated with my family at my father's funeral. He belonged there.

. . .

Meet with your minister, imam, rabbi, or whoever you want to conduct your funeral service. Talk to her or to him about who you want to eulogize you, what things you want to be certain are said and done, what you want to be sure is *not* said or done, who you want to carry your casket, what music you want played, and everything else you can think of to have peace of mind about the service. I will never forget Bobbie, who when I went to see her on the last day of her life summoned me close and whispered, "Rabbi, when you and the family come back here after the service, whatever you do, please, no deli! Make sure they have something classier." That was Bobbie. Wanting things to be special in life and no less so in death. I still laugh when I think about it, which is pretty much every time I am at a home after a funeral and there are deli platters on the table. But besides giving me a chuckle, Bobbie planned things to be as she wished rather than expecting people to know.

Here is one of the craziest examples of choosing to die the way you lived that I have ever heard of. Crazy, but also beautiful in its own way. The artist Jae Rhim Lee explained her unconventional plan in a Ted talk to a live audience:

I'm an artist, so I'd like to offer a modest proposal at the intersection of art, science, and culture. The Infinity Burial

Project, an alternative burial system that uses mushrooms to decompose and clean toxins in bodies. The Infinity Burial Project began a few years ago with a fantasy to create the Infinity Mushroom, a new hybrid mushroom that would decompose bodies, clean the toxins, and deliver nutrients to plant roots, leaving clean compost. But I learned it's nearly impossible to create a new hybrid mushroom. I also learned that some of our tastiest mushrooms can clean environmental toxins in soil. So I thought maybe I could train an army of toxin-cleaning edible mushrooms to eat my body.

So today, I'm collecting what I shed or slough off—my hair, skin, and nails—and I'm feeding these to edible mushrooms. As the mushrooms grow, I pick the best feeders to become Infinity Mushrooms. It's a kind of imprinting and selective breeding process for the afterlife. So when I die, the Infinity Mushrooms will recognize my body and be able to eat it. All right, so for some of you, this may be really, really out there.

. . . [But] I imagine the Infinity Mushroom as a symbol of a new way of thinking about death and the relationship between my body and the environment. See, for me, cultivating the Infinity Mushroom is more than just scientific experimentation or gardening or raising a pet, it's a step towards accepting the fact that someday I will die and decay. It's also a step towards taking responsibility for my own burden on the planet.

> *. . . Accepting death means accepting that we are physical beings who are intimately connected to the environment, as the research on environmental toxins confirms. And the saying goes, we came from dust and will return to dust. And once we understand that we're connected to the environment, we see that the survival of our species depends on the survival of the planet. I believe this is the beginning of true environmental responsibility.*

Crazy? Maybe. But that's a plan! Most of us won't take the extreme measure of a mushroom burial suit, but we should all consider the power of creating a death that reflects our life. Think about the jazz send-offs in New Orleans or the Irish wake, the twenty-one-gun salute, grandchildren placing notes in the casket. In Ghana people are buried in fantasy coffins. These coffins are a form of folk art that represent the deceased's vocation or something he or she loved to do in life. They range from a coffin shaped like a Mercedes-Benz for a business tycoon to an oversize fish for a fisherman to a really big Bible for someone who loved going to church. In the Philippines, the dead are sometimes buried in the hollow of a tree. In Tibetan culture, like many, bodies are considered empty vessels destined to return to the elements from which all life comes, and bodies are often cut into pieces and laid on a mountaintop for the birds to devour in what Tibetans call a sky burial. In the United States there is a company that will turn your body into a memorial "reef ball" by compressing your remains into a sphere that is attached to a reef in the ocean, providing a habitat for sea life. This, like the mushroom suit, might be too extreme for a lot of people, but the green burial movement has had an effect on the mainstream. In the United States, fewer people are choosing embalming and traditional concrete vaults, while biodegradable, woven-willow caskets or linen shrouds that decompose quickly into the earth are becoming more popular. Many cemeteries now have separate sections for these types of burials. People feel comforted knowing they will be honored by their loved ones in ways aligned with the values of their life.

Go to the cemetery if you wish to be buried in the ground or mausoleum and choose your gravesite. Meet with the mortuary and make all the decisions about whether you want a casket or would like to be cremated, what flowers you would like at the service, and what you would like to be dressed in; try to cover all the other questions the funeral director will want answered. Do this not only so that your death reflects your lived values, but also so that your loved ones will not have to guess what you wanted or endure the added stress of last-minute decision-making about things you could have resolved for yourself long before. Australian intensive care physician Peter Saul was right when he said, "Increasing longevity means more old age, not more youth." Use the fact that you will almost surely not die from a sudden event but rather from a slow decline as an opportunity; use that time and those years of accrued wisdom to take control over your own death. Make it a final, beautiful example of your life.

4

When More Is Not Better

If it be your will
That I speak no more
And my voice be still
As it was before
I will speak no more
I shall abide until
I am spoken for
If it be your will

—LEONARD COHEN,
"IF IT BE YOUR WILL"

I was tired and on my way home in terrible traffic from a clergy retreat in the California desert when the phone rang. It was Tara's husband, Dave. Tara wanted to see me right away. She wanted permission from me to kill herself.

Years of amyotrophic lateral sclerosis (ALS) had taken a terrible toll on Tara. It reduced her from a kick-ass attorney who had resolved some of the most complex divorce and custody cases imaginable; a funny, tough mom; a tall, striking woman; to what we all can imagine when we think of that cruel disease.

Tara did her homework when she was still mobile enough to see doctors and could still speak well enough to be understood. She knew what it took to get the aid-in-dying medication that is now legal in California. The details of this controversial law and her access to the life-ending medication are worth spelling out. The Coalition for Compassionate Care of California presents an informative precis of the End of Life Option Act. The law, whose intent is compassionate, is nevertheless written in words that are clinical and precise, cold and sobering—a reflection of our ambivalence about taking matters of life and death into our own hands:

OVERVIEW OF THE LAW

The End of Life Option Act is a California law that permits terminally ill adult patients with capacity to make medical decisions to be prescribed an aid-in-dying medication if certain conditions are met. Signed into law by

Governor Jerry Brown in October 2015, the law went into effect on June 9, 2016. California is the fifth state to enact an aid-in-dying law. . . .

To be eligible to request a prescription for the aid-in-dying drugs, an individual must:

- Be an adult (18 years old or older).
- Be a California resident.
- Have a diagnosis from his/her primary physician of an incurable and irreversible disease which will, within reasonable medical judgment, result in death within six months.
- Be able to make medical decisions for themselves as determined by health professionals.
- Voluntarily request a prescription for an aid-in-dying drug without influence from others.
- Be able to self-administer (eat, drink, and swallow) the aid-in-dying drug.

The request must be made solely and directly by the patient to the attending physician and cannot be made on behalf of the patient through a power of attorney, an advance health care directive, a conservator, health care agent, surrogate, or any other legally recognized health care decisionmaker. . . .

The Process for Requesting Aid-in-Dying Drugs

If a terminally ill patient meets the requirements to receive the aid-in-dying drug, the patient and his or her attending physician must follow several steps which are carefully defined in the law, including:

- The patient must make two oral requests, at least 15 days apart, directly to his or her physician (the attending physician).
- The patient must also make one request in writing, using the Patient's Request for Aid-in-Dying Drug form, which must be signed by the patient and two witnesses, and provided directly to his or her attending physician. The law does not say specifically when the written request must be made.
- The patient must discuss the aid-in-dying drug request with his/her attending physician without anyone else present (except an interpreter, if needed), to make sure the request is voluntary.
- The patient must then see a second physician (a consulting physician) who can confirm the patient's diagnosis, prognosis, and ability to make medical decisions.

If either physician thinks the patient's ability to make medical decisions could be impaired, the patient must also see a mental health specialist (psychiatrist or licensed psychologist) to make sure his or her judgment is not impaired.

The law requires that the patient and attending physician discuss all of the following:

- How the aid-in-dying drug will affect the patient, and the fact that death might not come immediately.
- Realistic alternatives to taking the drug, including comfort care, hospice care, palliative care, and pain control.
- Whether the patient wants to withdraw the request.
- Whether the patient will notify next of kin, have someone else present when taking the drug, or participate in a hospice program. (The patient is not required to do any of these things.)
- That the patient will not take the drug in a public location.

The physician must ensure the patient knows they do not have to take the drug, even once they have obtained the aid-in-dying drug.

If the patient still wishes to proceed and the attending physician agrees, the attending physician may provide the aid-in-dying drug by either dispensing it directly to the patient or by delivering the prescription to a participating pharmacist. By law, the physician cannot hand a written prescription directly to the patient or their representative.

The law is not specific about which aid-in-dying drug(s) can be prescribed.

Before taking the drug, the patient must sign a Final Attestation for Aid-in-Dying Drug form which confirms they are taking the drug voluntarily, are under no obligation to take the drug, and may rescind the request at any time. The completed form is to be returned to the attending physician to be placed in the patient's medical records.

Lawyer that she was, Tara had done it all according to the letter of the law.

"She won't do it, Rabbi, unless you tell her it is okay," Dave said to me before our call ended. "Get here as soon as you can. Please."

When I pulled up to the house, I saw the first indication of her debilitating disease, a wheelchair ramp at the front door. As I entered, there were more signs—countless bottles of pills, a wheelchair in the corner, stacks of adult diapers, masks, gloves, the special toilet seat from months before when Tara could still move around, the antiseptic smell of sanitizer. Most striking was the omnipresent feeling of someone's life receding, her presence shrinking from every room in the house except the master bedroom and bath, then shrinking further from there to the few square feet comprising the confines of a rented hospital bed, female urinal at the ready hanging off to the side. This was not living. This was dying and I knew it.

"Tara, the rabbi is here," Dave said loud enough to wake her from her exhausted slumber. Tara raised her head and took a slow, labored, shallow breath. Of all the many indignities of ALS, oxygen deprivation might be the cruelest. In 2020 the news was filled with terrifying stories about Covid-19, what it was like to suffer from that respiratory virus. Being barely able to draw enough breath to live, never being able to fill your lungs, feeling like you are drowning inside your own body—this is an awful form of suffering.

I could tell from her eyes that Tara was glad to see me, or at least relieved I had arrived. She could no longer speak, and a few days earlier had even lost the ability to point with her finger to the alphabet chart Dave would hold up for her to spell out simple words. She tried to tell me something, but it was impossible to understand what sounded not like words but grunts. There was not going to be any kind of nuanced dialogue about Tara ending her life. There would be no dialogue at all. Just a monologue. Just me.

"Rabbi," Dave said without any lack of clarity, "Tara asked me a few weeks ago to ask you when the time came whether or not she could take the pills. She wants to know now. She will do whatever you say."

As was true that time in my father's nursing home tossing him a balloon, I was again pulled between what I do and who I am. These two realities are the same most of the time. I am usually who I really am when I am showing up as the rabbi. But occasionally the rabbi and the man diverge, because the truth is, I am not always personally aligned with what religious law has to say about life and death. Sometimes I am torn, and this was one of those times. Did Tara ask Dave to summon me to her bedside because she wanted to know what the rabbi and therefore what Jewish law would say about her choosing to end her own life, or did Tara summon Steve Leder, the husband, the father, the man who had known her and her family for so many years, to find out what he thought she should do? There was no way for her to answer that question, and no way for me to answer it, either.

Of course, I could have taken the "on the one hand / on the other hand" approach that sometimes works. Just tell Tara what the tradition says pro and con. But she was too exhausted and in too much pain to appreciate the nuances of a legal argument. She just wanted to know, in a single word, if she could take the pills and kill herself. Yes or no?

My tradition is very clear about active euthanasia. It is wrong under all circumstances to hasten death. Our bodies are not really ours; we are not free to do with them as we please. They are God's, and only God can decide when a person should die. Rabbis are not supposed to play God; we are supposed to accurately relay the will of God as our tradition understands it. Some of this clarity comes from a famous story about the martyrdom of Rabbi Hanina ben Teradion, who was executed by the Romans in the second century because he ignored their prohibition against studying and teaching Judaism.

According to the nearly two-thousand-year-old account, the Romans took hold of Hanina, wrapped him in the Scroll of the Law, placed bundles of branches around him, and set them on fire. Then they brought tufts of wool, which they had soaked in water, and placed them over his heart, so that he would die a slower, more painful death. Apparently, despite this incredible cruelty, they had some measure of compassion for Hanina and urged him to open his mouth so that the smoke and fire would kill him more quickly. But Hanina refused by saying, "Let Him who gave me [my soul] take it away, but no one should injure oneself."

I was thinking about this story as I stood in front of Tara. I also remembered another Talmudic passage in which Rabbi Meir compares a dying person to a flickering lamp, in the sense that "the moment one touches it, one puts it out." This was the ancient sages' way of telling us that even when a person is actively dying, we should do nothing to hasten that death. A terminally ill patient, defined by Jewish law as someone expected to die within seventy-two hours, is considered a human being in all respects. Accordingly, anyone who kills such a person, even if that person is in extreme pain and very near death, is still considered a murderer. Suicide, which is another way of describing what Tara's taking the aid-in-dying drug would essentially be, is also explicitly forbidden by Jewish law for a terminally ill person. Bottom line, as one scholar put it, "no matter how hopeless or meaningless continued existence may appear to be in the eyes of the mortal perceiver, the life of a human being may be reclaimed only by the Author of life and death." Tara's life and death were in God's hands, not hers and not mine. Feeling the full weight of this law, I the rabbi would have to tell her no.

When a person dies, the first thing an observant Jew is instructed to say upon hearing the news is "Blessed be the Judge of Truth." In other words, we affirm the rightness of the death because we affirm it was God's decision. Whether or not it makes any sort of sense to us, we accept that cosmic justice and earthly justice might not be the same. This is also what the mourners are asked to say at the burial of their loved one when they tear the black ribbon pinned on their outer clothing. The tearing symbolizes our hearts torn by grief. It is a physical manifestation of the emotional. "Blessed be the Judge of Truth" has always been easy for me to ask mourners to say when the person who has died has lived a long life or has endured terrible pain or indignity of some kind that has mercifully ended. I translate the words for the mourners and follow by saying, "It was time for his suffering to end," affirming the rightness of the decree. Often they agree and repeat back to me, "Yes, it was time."

Even when it is the death of a child or a young parent and that death makes no sense at all, as a rabbi I tear those black ribbons and ask the brokenhearted mourners to repeat the Hebrew words for "Blessed be the Judge of Truth" after me, but I do not translate the words into English for them. I do what tradition technically requires of me, but I do not have to like it or force others to confront it fully. I just cannot bring myself to translate the words for the dear parents of that dead child or for those beautiful children of that parent now gone. I cannot bring myself to imply that all deaths, even inexplicable, tragic losses, are somehow the will of a benevolent God. But that is exactly what my tradition upholds. Life and death are in the hands of the Almighty. Tara should not take the pills. Rabbi Leder was obligated to say no.

But Steve Leder wanted to say yes. Steve Leder the human being wanted to say, "Tara, take the pills. It's okay. Your husband agrees, your kids agree, I agree." How could I be more compassionate with my dog when she was old, stricken with diabetes, blind, and in pain, I wondered, than Jewish law would allow me to be with Tara? Yes, there is every reason to prolong life, but as I looked into her pleading eyes and listened to her labored breath, I could not think of a single good reason to prolong Tara's death. As a rabbi, I have had that feeling so many times when leaving a nursing home or hospital room, the feeling that someone really would be better off dead. I know I felt that way when right before my father's funeral my parents' rabbi asked me to say those words as he tore the small length of black ribbon pinned on my suit coat. It made perfect sense to me as the rabbi and the son. By the end, there was almost nothing left of who my dad used to be; he was alive but not really living. Nothing would ever again make him laugh. He would never enjoy another meal; never again converse, walk, or have sex, or even have enough energy for anything other than slumping in his wheelchair.

During one of my father's many bouts of pneumonia my brother, Greg, said, "I hope he dies." I was shocked and awakened to the truth. He was right. Greg's head was clearer than mine in that moment; he was more my rabbi than I his. My dad survived that bout, but it was the day I knew in my heart that my powerful, fearsome dad was worn out. He was done. He eventually died peacefully in his sleep, so we never had to ask ourselves whether some contemplated measure would prolong his life or his death. But I knew that if that day ever arrived, my brother, Greg, had given me the clarity and the courage to know that Steve the son would do the right thing no matter what Steve the rabbi had learned in school.

When I am called into the ER or the ICU or the nursing home or the bedroom of a dying person by his or her family, in the midst of the sadness, the stress, and the chaos, I ask a single, simple question to cut through the emotional clutter: "Is what you are thinking of doing going to prolong his life or prolong his death?" It is loving to prolong life, to give someone a chance to live and love and laugh again. But it is cruel to prolong death.

No matter what I decided to say to Tara, I would not be in the room to witness the final moment of her life. Whatever the decision, I was getting into my car and driving home to hug my wife. But sitting next to Tara, I was imagining over and over again what it would be like to actually witness the ramifications of my decision. What is it like to be in the room with a person who is suffering so terribly that he or she is choosing that moment to die?

A few months later I received this email that answered my question. It was from my friend Mark, whose dad, Ted, was also a friend of mine for more than thirty years. I had helped Ted bury his wife three years before. Not long after that Ted's health declined dramatically. He was often in pain and exhausted and spoke of wanting to die nearly every day. Ted had

had enough of life. He was a retired attorney, and although in his nineties, he knew the law, including the End of Life Option law, and his son Mark did too. The day had arrived for Ted to end his life as he wished. This is how Mark described it:

The act of pushing so hard to get the meds, and the conversations, and the trainings and all that—I put aside my thoughts on the gravity of what I was doing and just focused on getting through it.

I went into the bathroom off the room where Dad was sitting. . . . I put on the mask and gloves and I mixed the meds. I went back into the room with my sister Rebecca, my dad, and the hospice nurse. I was in a trance. "Okay, here's what we're going to do. First, Daddy, do you still want to proceed? Do you understand what this means? Do you still want to go forward?" He nodded.

"Here are the steps . . . Is everyone ready?" Then I started the process of putting the meds in front of him because he had to take them. Legally, I couldn't "administer" them to him. After an hour of pre-meds, I brought him the final vial and said, "Daddy, once we start here, we have to move quickly. You need to drink this in under two minutes, okay? You ready?"

He grabbed the vial and just powered it down. You have to move quickly at this phase, as the dose must get in there or else the patient is unconscious but has not consumed quite enough to end it quickly. My dad was like a machine and got most of it down; then that massive, massive amount of barbiturates hit his bloodstream and there was an unexpected strong shudder and it was unreal as he fell back into his chair and was unconscious. His breathing wasn't labored, as is often the case with patients passing away under morphine. He was just—still. I held on to him tightly and kept my hand on his throat feeling his pulse. After maybe seven minutes I could feel nothing. The hospice nurse got out her stethoscope and confirmed.

At that point it just hit me that I had facilitated my father's death. What I had done was so totally irreversible and it was so abrupt, that space between talking to him and laughing and loving him to "he's gone." And he was gone because of what I had done.

All night Monday and all day Tuesday I was pretty wiped out and thinking over and over WTF had I done? The point of all this is that after talking to one of the agency counselors and to our friend Lisa (an internist for a lot of aging patients), I realized that I had the wrong perspective, totally the wrong perspective, and here's the really heavy shit but the piece that has allowed me to be free:

My dad knew this was an impossibly difficult thing to ask of someone, but he asked it of me. He knew that even with the emotion and the misery and the sheer terror of what I was going to have to do, he asked me to do it for him because he knew I would come through somehow, and help bring an end to what he was suffering. He was really struggling with what they call existential pain, and I totally get it. The humiliation I saw him endure and the horror of being trapped, unable to end what he prayed constantly would end, must have been unbearable. And he hid most of that with humor and sweetness. He never wavered and he made it clear to everyone that he wanted this and wasn't second-guessing anything, and he was at peace with his decision and was just praying it would be delivered to him. And he relied on me to help. He knew I would do it and he knew I would get through it.

From the BS paperwork hell, dealing with all the different doctors, the struggle to find the pharmacy, to the unreal experience of separating myself from the horror of mixing my own father's death, I understand now that I have to accept that he knew he'd taught me well. By all the wisdom and love and guidance with which he had nurtured me, and by the example he set through his whole life, he knew he'd formed me into someone that could get through this awful thing he'd asked me to do for him. But he didn't want it to be a burden that tormented me for the rest of my life. I'm starting to understand that he figured I'd become enough of a grown-up,

*and was certainly enough of a devoted son, that I would do it
and get through it, and then carry on.*

In that painful moment Mark knew what it meant to
honor his father. It was a moment of the deepest trust and
faith. It was as if all of Ted's life as a father and Mark's as a
son was preparation for that supreme moment. To love a person so much that for their own sake you let them go—that is
a powerful love. And for all of Mark's days yet to come, when
courage born of love is needed, he will summon his father
from within and allow that faith and love to guide him. It is
the beauty of what remains from the love of a father and a son.

We are raised to believe that if we make the right decisions
in life, there will be good outcomes, and that if we make the
wrong decisions, there will be bad outcomes. But oftentimes
that isn't really true. Most people who come to see me about
a problem have no *good* options, only bad and worse. Sometimes it is bad to get divorced but worse to stay married.
Sometimes it is bad to endure medical treatment but worse
not to; other times the opposite is true. In many ways, life is
not so clear or perfect as to give us good and bad. Tara had
only a bad and a worse option, and therefore so did I.

Again and again I have told people that when faced with
that very real question of whether you are prolonging your

loved one's life or your loved one's death, you will know the answer. The only question will be whether or not you have the courage to act upon what you know. The only question for me while sitting next to Tara, who was gulping for breath like a fish on land, was whether I was going to be Rabbi Leder or Steve Leder. In that moment, I could not find a way to be both. I held Tara's hand and searched her eyes. Which one had she summoned to her bedside, the rabbi or the son who out of the deepest love secretly wished his own father would die? Would she ever have imagined that sometimes they are not the same?

"Tara," I said, "you should take the pills." In that moment I violated my faith and confirmed my humanity.

It was a long, quiet drive home. Two hours later, Dave called to tell me Tara was dead. "Thank you, Rabbi Leder, for helping us," he whispered through his tears. But it was Lenny's son Steve who answered the phone.

5

Eulogies

The Universe is made of stories,
not of atoms.

—MURIEL RUKEYSER,
"THE SPEED OF DARKNESS"

A young man in my congregation was found dead in a shallow grave in the desert. Because he was a famous surfer, his parents asked that we gather on the beach to memorialize their son Bud before his surfing buddies paddled out into the Pacific to circle their boards, hold hands, and release flowers into the water in his honor. During the ceremony on the beach, one of his fellow surfers gave the eulogy. What he said shocked me a little and taught me a lot.

"When I first heard about Bud," he said in a Hawaiian surfer drawl almost too cliché to be true, "I was surfing Pipeline. I caught this huuuuge wave and it almost ripped my fuckin' head off. But I caught the lip, and I tuuuuubed it. And I just wanna say, it's 'cause Bud was with me."

It was forty-three words. It was raw in a way I thought was wrong and disrespectful at the time. But when I looked out at the front row filled with surfers all nodding their heads and wiping their eyes, I realized I was the one who was wrong.

Just as every culture has its rituals for saying goodbye, every spiritual leader has his or her way of guiding mourners on the path of letting go, of sorrow, of memory and truth; and each deserves respect. The first thing I do is arrange a time to meet with the family. Once the family is gathered, I tell them that we are going to do three things that day. The first is talk about any questions or unfinished details dealing with the mortuary and the cemetery. The second thing we are going to do is tell stories—as many as we'd like for as long as we'd like. There is so much I want to know. "We are going to make a big stew of stories," I tell them. And the third thing I want to do is walk them through exactly what is going to happen at the funeral from the moment they arrive at the cemetery to the moment they depart. "I can't make the funeral day easy," I honestly tell them, "but I can make it easier if you are prepared for what is going to happen." I tell the family what we are going to talk about because it gives them a sense of structure and direction. That is my most important objective when death visits a family—to structure the chaos of loss, letting them know consciously and subconsciously that there is a way through it all. This is my role; this is religion's role—to structure life and death in ways that make both meaningful.

Often, when a person dies, it is up to me to tell the story of that person's life. The family is either too heartbroken, too conflicted, or just too exhausted to eulogize their loved one themselves. I consider this one of the greatest honors bestowed upon me. But that does not make it easy. How do I do it? How do I distill a person's essence, his or her story, down to a few pages and a few minutes?

The process starts with that "big stew of stories." I say exactly that to the grieving family gathered in my study, weeping on my couch of tears. "There is a lot I want to know. So we are going to make a big stew of stories now. The happy, the sad, the funny, the embarrassing, the sweet, and the bitter. And we are going to tell those stories for as long as we feel like it and let things unfold however it seems best." I begin the conversation with the easiest questions first. Even if I knew the person who died really well and could answer the questions myself, I pose these simple questions regardless because they help people begin talking, sharing, and journeying back. Where was he born and when? What were his parents like? What did they do for a living? Did he have siblings? Did you ever hear any stories about him from when he was a little boy?

What kind of a kid was he? It is amazing to see how these initial questions help a family begin remembering the best of their loved one instead of simply experiencing the pain of loss.

Next, I begin moving toward the more intimate center of a person's life. If there is a surviving spouse, I will often ask her or him, "Do you remember the very first second that you laid eyes on each other?" The answer is always yes. "Where was it? What thought ran through your mind first?" The grieving spouse is instantly transported back to a time when he or she was young and felt that magical spark of true love that led to decades together. The adult children in the room are often amazed, a touch embarrassed, and filled with laughter to imagine their parents ever having had that kind of passion. "What? You thought Dad was a hottie? Really? Oh my God!" "Kids," those adult children say to their own children who are in the room, "cover your ears."

"What? Do you kids think you invented sex?" their grandmother might say.

By this point the children and grandchildren are moved, laughing, and delighted to journey back to a time before they were alive but that resulted in their very existence.

I keep inching toward the center. "Where was your first date? First kiss? When did you get engaged? Tell us the story." Next, to the adult children in the room I say, "Take us back to your earliest childhood memories of your dad. When you were just a little boy, when you were just a little girl, what was it like to be with him? What did you do together? Who was the disciplinarian, Mom or Dad? What pissed him off? Did he ever rescue you in some important way? What of your dad's character do you see in yourself?" I am interested in their adult perspective about their parents' marriage. What was the vibe like? Tell me about their love for each other.

Then I'll say, "Suppose I said to your dad, not recently when he has been so ill, but let's say twenty years ago when he was feeling great, 'You have all day and all night to do whatever you want. You have no responsibilities at all.' How would he have spent that day and night? What did he really love to do? What made him happy?" This allows everyone in the room to remember their loved one before age and disease took their toll; before the Alzheimer's or the chemo, before the doctors and the needles and the tests and the tubes.

There is an old Yiddish expression that says, "A half-truth is a whole lie." So next I go deeper still. "So far, he sounds perfect. But no one is perfect. What wasn't so perfect about him?" Eyes dart back and forth as if to say without words, "Can we, should we, talk about this in front of the grandchildren and the rabbi? In front of one another? In front of Mom?"

"It's okay," I offer gently. "We all have flaws. What were his flaws?" This moment allows a family to express a whole truth about a whole person—the regrets, the shortcomings and mistakes of their loved one's life.

Not long ago there was a media scandal in the wake of Kobe Bryant's death in a helicopter crash. The scandal was the result of *CBS This Morning* anchor Gayle King's interview with WNBA star Lisa Leslie. Kobe was the greatest basketball player of his generation and did a lot of great things in his retirement too. But like all of us, he was human and flawed. From a public standpoint, his deepest flaw was revealed when Bryant reached an out-of-court settlement with a nineteen-year-old accuser who claimed he had raped her. Kobe initially lied to investigators and denied having sex with his accuser. When the officers said they had physical evidence, Bryant admitted to having sexual intercourse with her. He also admitted to strangling her during sex, as the accuser had bruises on her neck. He was married at the time.

Gayle had interviewed me for the launch of a previous book, and we had exchanged a number of emails after Charlie Rose was fired at the beginning of the #MeToo movement, just a day after he and Gayle had interviewed me. In her interview with Lisa Leslie, Gayle said Kobe Bryant's legacy was "complicated," and she went on to ask Leslie if her feelings for her basketball mentor had been affected by the incident. What followed was a blistering attack on Gayle, including death threats from Kobe fans who thought the question was mean-spirited and inappropriate. It was a sad example of how cruel and cowardly people can be when hiding behind the curtain of social media. I immediately emailed Gayle and told her I wanted her to know that her rabbi friend believed in her and believed her question was right and fair. I told her how, whenever I sit down with a family to prepare for the funeral of their loved one, I ask a lot of questions, and one of them is *always* about the person's flaws. If you don't ask that question, you don't get the true picture of a person. I told her: "You did the right thing."

It might seem counterintuitive, but pretending a person was perfect at his or her funeral often makes the family feel worse, not better—as if the funeral were a kind of theater piece that they were knowingly a part of. A show. A scam. Of course, this truth-telling has to be done artfully in the context of a eulogy. There is an old Hebrew expression that in English means "Those who know will understand." In other words, seek a way to say difficult things about someone that those in the know will recognize as truth yet those on the outside will simply perceive as a benign observation or even a compliment. For example, if someone was intrusive to a fault in her children's lives—always questioning their choices, often voicing criticism, and so forth—I might lay that out in a eulogy by saying, "Many years ago a friend of mine told me that the worst thing a parent could be was indifferent. As a mother, she was never indifferent." Those who know how intrusive she was will know what I am saying and that it is true. They might laugh, they might simply nod their heads, but they will know that I am articulating an important truth, and that truth validates the family's feelings. Others who don't know will think only that she cared deeply about her children.

If a man was harsh as a father, at times frightening and mean, I can tell that truth as sensitively as possible by saying something like "It wasn't always easy to be his son. He could be tough on you. But that toughness was born of him wanting the best for the people he loved most." This is the art of allowing a family its truth; of allowing them to feel heard without embarrassing them, outing them, or being unnecessarily damning of the deceased. Truth-telling at the time of loss is so important. Yes, with sensitivity and compassion, but the truth nevertheless really does set the mourners free, whether that truth is good or bad or both. And it is always both for every one of us.

The stew of stories, the upcoming funeral, and all the years to follow are a reckoning with the entire truth of a person's life and our relationship with that person in all of its complexity. I tell the family to trust me with the truth; that I will handle it deftly during the funeral. They almost always do open up about their loved one's flaws—the stubbornness, the business mistakes, the addiction, the distance the person put between himself or herself and those he or she claimed to love. The truth, when spoken, lifts the weight of a secret. The truth is a blessing.

Sometimes the truth is something we would rather avoid completely. I will never forget the time I drove into the cemetery, parked in the space behind the chapel reserved for clergy, and saw my friend who ran the mortuary waiting for me to step out of the car. "Hey, do you want to see the pantyhose?" he asked. He knew by the look on my face that I had no idea what he was talking about. "I guess no one told you, did they?"

"Told me what?" I asked.

He then went on to tell me that the man I was about to bury died at home from autoerotic sex gone wrong while dressed as a woman in pantyhose. I was shocked because when we met for the intake meeting his sons had told me only that he died at home in his study after a heart attack. Of course, I went ahead with the funeral and eulogy I had planned, but I was sad inside. I knew that his sons were keeping a secret that I could have helped them to accept. I knew their dad, and he was a wonderful guy, a doctor who cared deeply for his patients. I could have helped them process the truth of his secret life during our conversation earlier that week in a way that might have unburdened them. I could have said something in his eulogy that would have let them know

I empathized with them and at the same time not let on to anyone else what the circumstances of their father's death really were. Perhaps something as simple as "He was in many ways a very private person who died in a very private way." Something, anything, to let his sons put down the weight of their secret.

Secrets are bad for a family and a community, even after death. If the death was an overdose, I find a way to say it. "Hard as she tried, and that was very, very hard, she had demons she just could not slay and her pain was too great to bear." If the death was a suicide, that too ought to be said. My rabbi friend Ronne, whose son Jesse died by suicide, said it as directly and movingly as anyone could when he eulogized Jesse.

> *Let me begin with the fact, the worst, unremitting, irrevocable fact: Jesse took his own life. No one need speak the word suicide in a whisper or avoid direct reference to it when speaking of him or to us. It was what he did, but it was not who he was. He had struggled intermittently with ideation of suicide for at least ten years and chose the least violent, least dramatic means that he could conceive. It was not a retributive act against anyone; it simply was, for him, in the end, the inescapable escape.*

We shall not attempt to pursue beyond the silence. We acknowledge that we will never see the fulfillment and joy that we wished most for Jesse. We pray that with the help of loving family and friends and with the grace of God, we will relearn how to live. We pray that our love for Jesse might not disappear with him, but instead be transmuted so that we may be restored to lives of purpose and service. If there is anything to be said, in the end, it is just this: the pain of our loss is the greatest evidence we can offer of the importance and meaning of life.

I do not know whence Ronne summoned the strength to speak that truth, but his courage, his honesty, and his heart are the finest example of truth-telling in a eulogy I have ever witnessed.

For me, there is nothing more difficult, draining, or important than supporting a family through the death of a young child. That too involves the telling of truths. I talk about how frightening it is to all of us who have children, how heartbreaking and unjust it is. I look those parents right in the eyes and tell them that I know they also want to die from this pain, but that we cannot die because children die, we can only live to honor them and their memory. I promise them in everyone's presence that things will not always hurt so and that we will never stop loving them and that we will never forget.

Here is what I often say at the beginning of a eulogy for a young person who has died or an adult who dies suddenly, leaving his or her family in shock. These particular words were for a husband and father who died suddenly.

Our hearts ache this afternoon. This surreal, sad afternoon, we begin to move forward with the impossible but real truth that Jimmy is physically gone from us. It is impossible to believe that we are here this afternoon at his funeral . . . and yet we know that we are. It is absurd, yet it is so. And it is so, so painful.

How could a life force as charming, kind, hilarious, loving, laughing, collecting, dealing, sweet, brave, crazy, tough, and beautiful as Jimmy be gone? I am sorry for the pain that all of you who knew and loved him are facing today and will face for many days to come. I am especially sorry for you, Jimmy's beautiful family—a family I care very much about. I am sorry for the surrealness of it all; for the confusion, the regret, the exhaustion, and the hurt.

But this pain is our pain, this confusion our confusion, this sadness our sadness, not Jimmy's. The ancient rabbis said death, even at its worst, is only "perfect sleep." Jimmy is now beyond sadness and loss, confusion, regret or pain. Jimmy is at rest. And Jimmy is at peace. And we can all at least be grateful

*for and take some measure of comfort in the rest and the peace
that he so much deserves.*

When death is unforeseen and tragic, it is excruciatingly
painful for those who mourn. But for the dead, it is a death
like all others—perfect sleep. The deepest peace.

If it is the death of a young parent, I look at those sad
children and I tell them, "Your mother loved you and she will
always love you. And all of us who care, all of us who loved
her will help you carry this terrible sadness and we will help
you remember her and she and we will be here with you until
the day that you feel joy again in your heart and every day
after that for the rest of your lives."

When this truthful, beautiful, painful, laughter- and tear-
filled storytelling with a family is near an end, I ask two final
questions, prefacing both by acknowledging that they are difficult questions. By this point, there is generally a lot of trust
between us, a lot of truth and love in the room. The first of
these questions goes something like this: "I know that you
have already thought a lot about what I am going to ask you
next. When you think about life going forward without your
loved one's physically being a part of it, what do you think you
are going to miss the most?" If the answer is "everything," I
gently push a little harder. We may miss everything, but we

also miss some things more intensely and some things more frequently than others after we lower a loved one into the ground.

I have learned from my own father's death that often the things we miss the most are seemingly small and insignificant and yet so emblematic of who that person was and always will be within us. When I am eating something delicious, when I am wiping my plate clean with a crust of bread, when I learn a new joke I know he would have loved but can't call him to make him laugh, when the lilacs bloom on his birthday each May, when I raided the neighbor's lemon tree during the Covid-19 crisis because the grocery store ran out, when I am listening to someone arrogant tell me what he thinks (I can hear my father saying in Yiddish "*chochem* [wise guy]," with a knowing wink), when I am walking in the sun—no one I know has ever loved the sunshine more than my dad. These are the moments when I miss my dad the most.

Finally, I ask what I think is the most powerful of all questions because it gives voice back to the deceased, allowing him or her to complete the story. I have always believed in giving the last word to the dead. "Let's assume for a moment that he was here with us during this entire conversation. In a way he has been, because we have brought him to life with these stories, but I mean this literally. Let's assume he was hiding over there underneath the desk listening to our entire conversation. Then we finish, you leave, and Dad steps out from under the desk and says, 'Rabbi, I heard what everyone had to say about me and I don't dispute a single word of it. It was all true. But this is what I want you to say tomorrow to my family and friends and their friends who will be at the funeral.'"

In other words, I ask the family, "If he could be there tomorrow with all of you, if he could stand up there and look out at you and say something, what do you think it would be?" There is almost always a still moment of silence followed by someone saying, "I know exactly what he would say," and then everyone chimes in. When I write the eulogy I often choose to end with those answers, which in a sense brings the deceased back to life again at his or her own funeral for a final spoken goodbye. And those imagined last words are always an exquisitely beautiful, brief truth—the crystalline distillate of a person's story, a legacy of love.

A family's storytelling before a funeral always creates an amazing transformation—from tears to tears and laughter; from hopelessness to the certainty that we live on through memory; from the pain of isolation to the kinship of family. It is life in the midst of death.

From all of this, I create a eulogy. Not an obituary, but a eulogy. An obituary tells the facts of a person's life. A eulogy reveals the truths of a person's life, a person's true story.

The eulogy I felt most privileged to write was the one for my own father. The ten years he battled Alzheimer's gave me a lot of time to think about what I would say when he died, because in a way I was watching him die a little each time I visited. Each time I traveled from Los Angeles to Minneapolis and to the nursing home where he lived, I found him more diminished. As the man he was evaporated, that diminishment revealed not only what I missed and would never have again, but also the remaining beautiful essence of who my father really was underneath the topography and details of his life.

I knew the well-meaning young rabbi of my parents' synagogue would someday gather our family together to tell him my father's story. I knew we would cry and laugh and journey back to who my dad was before the Alzheimer's took him away. I knew my mother would remain mostly silent. I knew the rabbi would then go home to write a handful of paragraphs about my dad to follow whatever I had to say at the funeral. And I knew he could never get it right.

People often ask me how I manage the difficulty of writing a eulogy for someone I didn't know. They are usually surprised when I tell them that writing a eulogy for a person I didn't know is much easier than writing one for someone I did. If I never knew the person, I need only structure the memories of his or her family and friends into a narrative arc.

As long as I organize and accurately reflect their perspectives, they feel the story has been well told. But if I really knew a person, then I also know if I am getting the eulogy exactly right or not. It is much more difficult to be accurate when you know the full truth. Writing my father's eulogy was going to be the singular, hopefully beautiful moment I had spent my life preparing to embrace—every writing class, every speech class, every school play, every family stew of stories, and every eulogy I had ever written for others was preparation to tell the truth of my father's life and of mine.

When my father lost most of his ability to speak, he would smile when I walked in the room. "I have to remember to tell people about how his eyes seem even bluer when he smiles," I would tell myself. When I would push him in his wheelchair on the path surrounding the lake near the nursing home, we would pause to watch a kid reel in a fish. It took me back to when my dad would take me fishing on Sunday mornings. Watching him row the boat—shirtless, tan, relaxed, happy even—made me feel like I had the strongest dad in the world, like I was safe and he loved me because he was with me. He did all the dirty work—worms, hooks, guts—and taught me not to fear the gore of it all. "I have to remember to talk about fishing with my dad." When I watched my mom spoon-feed him his pureed food and wipe his chin like a baby in a high chair, I thought to myself, *She is doing her duty, despite the many times she hated him as a husband. How will I ever deal honestly with their marriage in his eulogy?* For a decade, Steve the rabbi was taking notes for the eulogy Steve the son would someday write.

You might think that helping so many people through loss, death, and grief would be a terrible burden. Sometimes it is. Sometimes I come home tired and sad. Sometimes I cringe when the answering service calls me in the middle of the night because I just don't think I can show up again so soon to carry another family's pain. There are many early mornings or late evenings when I say to Betsy, "I have to write a eulogy now. I hate my job. Who willingly walks into rooms so full of other people's pain? I need to retire. I am burnt out. I wish they would ask for one of the other rabbis."

Yet despite how hard it can be, guiding all those families through making that stew of stories has taught me so much— not about death, but about life. Writing so many eulogies has given me lessons in how to live my life as a son, a brother, a husband, a father, a rabbi, and a friend. I know now how I want my family to answer the questions I ask other families in the wake of death when the person doing the asking will be some other rabbi, and I will be no more. I have learned that loved ones remember and miss the seemingly little things the most—the things that made them laugh or the times we showed up to rescue them with a simple hug, letting them know they were not alone. Walks on the beach, a game of catch, a day fishing on the sun-dappled water, a loan when you were broke, a date to get your nails done together, ice cream on a hot summer night, a smile when you walked in the room. Mostly what I have learned from listening to so many stories of a person's life set against the backdrop of death is that life and love are essentially about time—time spent consciously, deliberately, mundanely, lovingly together when you could otherwise have been apart.

Most people think that the rabbi, minister, imam, family members, or friends write the eulogy for a person who has died. But do we really? Did I really create my father's eulogy or anyone else's over all these years? The answer, of course, is no. The profound and simple truth is that we are each writing our own eulogies every day with the pen of our lives.

6

The Last Goodbye

*Ah, if you knew what peace
there is in an accepted sorrow!*
—CELIA PARKER WOOLLEY,
THE WESTERN SLOPE

"Now, let's talk about the funeral tomorrow," I usually say when I feel the stew of stories has simmered to perfection, or I have to get to my next meeting soon (there is that splinter of ice again). It is time for me to walk the family through the details of the coming day—when to arrive, where to park, where to sit, who will speak and in what order, who will bear the casket—all the choreography of death.

Death forces us to let go of the physical. Buddhists study, meditate, and work at embracing impermanence their entire lives. For the rest of us—and perhaps even for them—it is numbing, painful, frightening, surreal, and strange to be in the presence of a dead body and to return that body, whether whole or in ash, to the earth and the elements. I have seen more than a thousand dead bodies, and it is clear that the body is not the person—that there is so much more to us than our corporeal being. It is the impermanence of the body that has convinced me of the eternality of the soul. Physics tells us that energy never dies, it merely assumes a different form. I never feel this more deeply than when gazing upon a dead body, a vessel emptied of its life force, a force that must surely now exist elsewhere.

Just before my father's funeral service began, the rabbi walked me and my family into the chapel the way I have walked so many families into facing death for so many years. In that moment I understood how the rabbi felt, but I did not understand how I felt. We were ushered into the front row. I sat, Betsy at my side, our children, Aaron and Hannah, there too, and I could do nothing, nothing but sink my head in my hands, bent over, and weep. I did not want to be there. I did not want to believe that we were about to begin the funeral of my dad. We were going to bury him and there was nothing, nothing I could do to stop it.

He did not look like himself in the casket, although maybe he did. We put suits and ties or dresses on the dead. We put makeup on the dead. All of this is to make them look less dead, and I wanted him to be less dead, but he would never, ever be less dead, only more dead. Only then did I understand how all of the thousands of people I have helped at funerals felt at that very moment when I was with them to bury their loved one—surreal, empty. I was there, but not there, and there was nothing, nothing I could do.

We have sanitized death to an unprecedented degree. Our loved ones mostly do not die at home, and even if they do, very quickly a van arrives from the mortuary to whisk their body away, drain it of blood, fill it with preservatives, and cover it with cosmetics, and we do not see it again until the funeral. Modern embalming dates back to the Civil War, which lasted much longer and was far bloodier than most people anticipated at the time. More than six hundred thousand men died in that war, nearly half of all the soldiers who have died in all of America's wars. The Civil War created a new professionalized culture of death and mourning. Hundreds of thousands of men were dying far from home. Embalmers followed battles the way tow truck drivers now listen to police scanners and show up after car accidents. Some embalmers even propped up bodies in front of their tents as a way to advertise their services. They also profited from death by selling expensive caskets to the soldiers' families who could afford it; the casket was used to encase the embalmed body for the train ride home and burial to follow.

The embalming business became a permanent part of American culture when President Lincoln's body was embalmed and placed on a funeral train for a tour of one hundred and eighty cities. Until little more than a century ago most people died at home. Their bodies were washed and prepared for burial by people who loved them. This business of being transported after death quickly away from the living and then chemically altered to seem somehow less dead has made it more difficult, not less, for mourners to embrace the reality of death. While I have had considerable experience with death over all my years as a rabbi, I also found it hard to believe what I was seeing as I gazed upon my dead father.

The rabbi uttered his first words, but I did not, could not, look up. My head on my knees, for the first time in my life I understood what the psalmist meant and felt when he said, "I am bent and bowed low" (Psalm 38:6).

Like all traditional Jewish mourners, we tore the small black ribbon pinned to our chests and said the words *Baruch Dayan HaEmmet*—Blessed be the Judge of Truth. This is the starkest of admissions that the time of death is not ours to decide. It really is in God's hands. Life ends, and we cannot change that. Not with love, not with strength, not with science, not with faith, not with anything. Death wins, always. And it tears us apart inside. Deeper still there is the realization that if the person you loved so deeply is mortal, then you too are mortal and shall someday surely die.

When I was a boy, my dad would often introduce me to

others with a wink, a smile, and the words "You'd never guess whose son this is." To say I resembled him would be putting it mildly. I think it made him proud. I was definitely his. Occasionally my aunts would show me pictures of my dad when he was young, and we would marvel at the similarities. Now, at sixty years old, when I look in the mirror, I feel as if my father is staring back at me. The bags under my eyes, the tip of my nose, my cheeks, my neck, the little bulge in my belly—they are all his. Once I was with my mother in my father's room at the nursing home. She told me that he had something akin to diaper rash on his penis and so they had left him naked from the waist down, lying on a pad, until the rash cleared up. "Go look," she said. I didn't want to. Why would I? But for reasons I will never really understand, my mother was unusually insistent. Was she making me do it to bear witness to his helplessness or to diminish my father in his son's eyes? Was she merely concerned about his rash, wanting me to commiserate? "I mean it," she said. "Look." I lifted the sheet and looked at my father's penis for the first time since I was very young. It looked like mine. Even after officiating at a thousand funerals, I never truly felt my own mortality until my father died and I saw him in that casket. As I stared at him in that plain pine box, it hit me with surreal yet near perfect clarity. My life too would someday end, and I was going to look just like him when I was dead.

That simple, stark realization has helped me move forward in fulfilling some of my lifelong dreams. It convinced me to spend money to build a small getaway in the Mojave Desert, where I can escape with only my family into the anonymity and the quiet of the desert. My father's death saddened me, but it also propelled me to take my time on earth and my life more seriously. Time, life, and we are finite. We really are only human. We can each do only so much, control only so much, and at some point we have to let go, trust, live. To be at peace with our helplessness is the most terrible and liberating of lessons.

There are many ways to say goodbye, to remember, to celebrate the soul's passing on to some different level of existence, whatever that may be. The Hebrew word for funeral is *l'vayah*—it comes from the verb "to accompany." We the living see ourselves as accompanying the deceased as he or she moves from one realm of existence to another, whatever and wherever that may be. The social distancing restrictions during the Covid-19 pandemic showed me in stark relief just how beautiful it is to be surrounded by people who care when it is time to mourn. Imagine a funeral where only one household of mourners, not exceeding ten people, are allowed to attend. Everyone is behind face masks. All are seated ten feet apart, and no one is allowed to carry the casket or to place earth into the grave or to hug another. No stew of stories with me in their home or in my office beforehand, no gathering with family and friends after. Just Zoom—distant and sterile, adding yet another surreal layer to an already strange journey through death. Very often, when sitting with a family the day before a funeral, I could look them in the eyes and honestly say, "I know you don't believe it, but tomorrow is going to help. You will feel, even if just a little, that after a day of being surrounded by your family and friends who care and who remember, the clouds begin to lift." During the pandemic, I couldn't say that, because I didn't think it was true. To me, under those terrible circumstances, it seemed that the funeral did little if anything to help. What it did was reaffirm my faith in the importance and healing power of time-tested customs of togetherness under more usual circumstances.

I always begin a funeral service by teaching a brief lesson about and then reciting the Twenty-Third Psalm. Most of us have recited it at a funeral:

> *The Lord is my shepherd; I shall not want. He makes me lie down in green pastures.*
> *He leads me beside still waters. He restores my soul.*
> *He leads me in paths of righteousness for His name's sake.*
> *Even though I walk through the valley of the shadow of death,*

I shall fear no evil, for You are with me; Your rod and Your
  staff, they comfort me.
You prepare a table before me in the presence of my enemies;
You anoint my head with oil; my cup overflows.
Surely goodness and mercy shall follow me all the days of
  my life,
and I shall dwell in the house of the Lord forever.

I point out in my opening remarks that one reason this psalm is recited almost universally at Jewish and Christian funerals is obvious. In it, the psalmist imagines death as a sort of peaceful eternal existence, like lying in a green pasture beside still waters—a beautiful metaphor for the deepest peace. But there are two more nuanced and very powerful reasons I think this psalm has become so much a part of funerals and memorials. They are both found in the familiar verse "Even though I walk through the valley of the shadow of death, I shall fear no evil, for You are with me." First, the poet reminds us that we can and will walk through the dark valley that is death and grief. We do not stay in darkness forever. With time, with memory, with prayer, with candles, with stories retold, with reaching out and reaching in, we find a way back into the light. We can be scarred forever, but still, we can summon an amazing capacity to move forward despite our very real losses and pain. We do not die because people we love die. Nearly all of us somehow find a way to walk through the valley, we do not remain there forever.

But getting through it is not even the most profound meaning to be found in the metaphor of the valley of the shadow of death. For what is a shadow really, but proof of light? A shadow can exist only because of light that—even if partially obstructed by a mountain, a tree, or our grief—somehow nevertheless still shines. A shadow cannot exist without light. Love is that light, shining through memory, illuminating and reminding me of so many things about my dad; reminding each of us who mourn of a love absent and yet still present, still warm and aglow even when skies are gray.

Next, I often share an old story to try to help people understand why we gather for a funeral. On the surface of it, it's just a simple tale about two large ships, one entering the harbor, the other leaving. According to the story, a huge crowd on the pier was giving the outgoing ship a tremendous send-off, while the incoming ship slipped into the harbor entirely unnoticed. A sage on the pier scolded the crowd, saying, "Don't celebrate the ship setting out to sea. You have no idea what destiny awaits it." Pointing to the incoming vessel, he said, "Turn around, notice, appreciate, and celebrate that ship that has traveled so well and so long and finally come home safely."

Of course, this is not a story about two ships at all. It's a story about birth and death. When a baby is born, everyone celebrates, although the truth is that we have no idea what destiny awaits that child as it makes its way through life. And it is also true that when a person dies, we often express mostly sorrow and remorse. The ancient sages who told that tale were trying to teach us that we often have things backward. The life to be appreciated, uplifted, and celebrated is the life of a person who has traveled well and long through both stormy waters and calm, beautiful seas, and has finally arrived home safely. I use this story not in the rare instances of tragic or premature death, but for the far more common death of someone who has lived a long and full life. I use the story to remind everyone there that the stories we are about to tell are a reflection of a beautiful life and legacy—a successful journey to be celebrated despite our tears.

I recently came across another metaphor for life and death that I love. It's modern and involves a car instead of two ships, and it's every bit as true. A friend of mine read it at his father's funeral after he poured some whiskey into the grave. "Life is not a journey to the grave with the intention of arriving safely in a pretty and well-preserved body. The goal is to skid in broadside; tires smoking, body all dented, leaking fluids, and your fuel gauge on empty; thoroughly used up and worn out, and loudly proclaiming, 'Holy shit, what a ride!'"

· · ·

After the eulogies have been delivered, there is a final physical letting go, the carrying and the lowering of the casket. The turning of the spade. The thunk of earth on wood or metal six feet below. This is often more beautiful than one might think. Take, for example, these reminiscences of the writer Marcie Hershman, which appeared in *The New York Times*. It wasn't until her grandmother's death that she really learned what it meant to carry a loved one with love.

When she was a little girl, it was, of course, her grandmother who carried her.

"Put your foot right on top of mine," she'd say. "That's good, mamelah. *Now come stand on me with the other one."*

"But doesn't it hurt you, Nanny?"

"Hurt me?" With a laugh she smoothed the loose strands of blond hair into my ponytail. "Why, you're so light, you weigh nothing. You're like a pinch of air. Other foot on top, come on—up! That's good; balance on me. And put an arm around my waist so no one falls."

. . . Clinging to her wide, warm, familiar body, giggling and gasping, I spun with my grandmother in giant circles across the dark parquet floor of the living room. Occasionally I slid off her feet (my anklet socks wouldn't hold), but I always

scrambled right back. We danced on and on, unequal partners who in those moments absolutely loved all the inequalities about us, the jokiness, the seriousness. My grandmother was singing; her voice was loud and clear. She spun me for a long time. Our heads thrown back, legs stepping, arms pumping, our fingers intertwined.

Years later it was Marcie's turn to carry her grandmother.

"Now," said the funeral director, with a nod. And at that signal we lifted the casket. It was—she was—so light. She weighed nothing, like a pinch of air. I'd been afraid that I wouldn't be able to hold her up. . . . But, really, she was so light, held by the six of us. I had no idea it would feel like this to be a pallbearer: Gentle. Cradling. Maternal. . . .

Watching from the sidelines of the burial processions of others I'd loved in the past, I'd never known how the loving kindness in the act overflowed, how it returned to fill the hearts of those who raised the casket and carried it to its measure of earth.

I'd thought of pallbearing as gloom, oppressiveness, darkness, a struggle to remain upright under both a physical and atmospheric—an impossible—weight. That narrow box of a world with all light extinguished, all weight given over, yielded only effort and loss. Pallbearing was connected to destruction.

We lifted—and my arm was pulled downward, but that was all. As we slowly moved into the wind, I didn't buckle. For how absolutely steady Nanny's last weight was; how perfectly still. How little it asked of me. Only that I carry her gently. As so many times she had on her own carried me.

That's really all they ask of us—our parents; our lovers, husbands, and wives; our children and dear friends. That we carry them gently in our lives as they carried us in theirs. Not with crushing sadness, for they do not wish such weight upon us. But with lightness and warmth.

God bless them for the memories they left for us that make carrying them with joy possible. The wisdom and love they bequeathed us. The joy and comfort they brought to us as they carried us through life so that now we might carry them forever in our hearts—without bitterness, without crushing sadness. When someone has loved us well and long, we need not buckle beneath the weight of sorrow. Instead, we can carry them with us with gratitude, completeness, and joy.

And what about us? Are we learning the lesson about life that our loved ones' deaths have come to teach us? What are we leaving behind for our own families and friends to carry with them when we are gone? For just as surely as we carry the people we love, so too will we be carried by the people who love and remember us. Will they carry in their hearts and minds' eyes the certain knowledge of our unfailing love? Will we leave behind for them memories of laughter, wisdom, goodness, and generosity? Will their memories of us bring them joy? Funerals are a profound reminder that our loved ones will carry us in death only as gently and lovingly as we carried them in life.

"Put your foot right on top of mine," Marcie's grandmother would say, "Other foot on top, come on—up! That's good; balance on me. And put an arm around my waist so no one falls. That's good, mamelah. That's good."

If there will be young children at a funeral, I spend some time talking with their parents about how to prepare them. I begin by encouraging them to include their young children in the day's events. If a child is old enough to remember not being allowed to attend a parent's, a grandparent's, or another loved one's funeral, they should be there. Otherwise, they are learning to distance themselves from death and people who are grieving instead of learning to show up. Children do not naturally fear funerals. They learn that fear from adults. When there are young children at funerals whose parents have not instilled fear in them, they are very present. They want to see everything up close, even to the point of taking my hand and walking right up to the grave to look in, to watch the casket being lowered, to participate in the placing of earth upon it. They are not afraid and will be only if we are.

I remind parents to prepare their children by telling them that they might hear loud crying at the funeral, but that crying is okay and that feeling sad is okay. I warn against ever saying that the person who died was "sick" or is "sleeping," because all children get sick and all children go to sleep, and we do not want them to fear that either of those things mean they are dying. Say instead, "He had something happen to his body that the doctors could not fix. Doctors can almost always fix our bodies, but sometimes, especially when we are very, very old, they can't." Instead of saying he is sleeping, say that his body has died and is being returned to the earth, but (assuming you believe this) there is another part of him that we call the soul (or the spirit or whatever word you prefer); that's the part we remember in our hearts, and that part of him is still with us whenever we remember him. The metaphor of a caterpillar, a cocoon, and a butterfly can help children make sense of this. In life we are made up of a body and a soul, like a caterpillar living in a cocoon. When we die, the body releases our soul like the cocoon releases a beautiful butterfly. If your child offers his or her own theory, no matter how wacky or different it is from your own beliefs, it is best not to challenge him or her directly by saying, "That's not true" or "I don't believe that." It is much better to say, "That's an interesting idea. Some people believe that," and then go on to give your child other ideas that you believe might be more helpful by adding, "And other people believe . . ."

Days, weeks, or months after attending a funeral, parents should expect children to fear that their parents will die. They may or may not voice the fear, but it is very often there. What do we say when a child asks his or her parents, "Are you going to die?" We should tell children the truth, but in a way that comforts them. Tell them, "Yes, all living things die—the leaves on trees and eventually the trees themselves, flowers, pets, and people. But I am not going to die until I am very old, like Papa was. And before then, here are some of the things that are going to happen first. You are going to grow up more. You will turn sixteen and be able to drive a car. Then when you are eighteen, you will finish high school and go to college. Then you will finish college and choose what you want to do for your job. Then you will have a job and earn money and live in your own home. Then hopefully you will meet someone and fall in love. You might decide to get married, and then, after a while, you might decide to have a baby and you will be the mommy and I will be the grandma, and it won't be until all those things have happened and I am very, very old that my time will come to die."

As an adult, you know there might be an exception to any of the things you just said. Some people do die suddenly and prematurely. Some people do not grow up to marry or have their own children. But telling your child that you will not die until you are very, very old and he or she is well prepared for life, despite the slim chance it might be otherwise, is no different from telling a young child that the plane is not going to crash. We all know that the plane actually could crash, though this is quite unlikely; so unlikely that it's not something you need to share with a child.

I hope the death of a grandparent is not the first time you have helped your children experience death in a healthy way. When your child's fish, hamster, lizard, or hermit crab dies, this is an opportunity to help him or her learn about how to approach death. Don't flush the fish! Don't run out and buy another to replace it and hope your child won't realize that the first fish died. A fish funeral is a great chance to prepare the body (a matchbox works well), have a brief service during which everyone in the family can gather around a hole dug in the yard and share their favorite memories of the fish, then gently lower it into the ground, cover it, and perhaps even plant a flower or tree above it as a memorial. I know someone who lost her first pet, a gerbil named Herbie (short for Herbivore), when she was six or seven. Her father, an avid gardener, helped her bury Herbie in the garden bed beneath her bedroom window. Then they planted giant sunflowers that grew as tall as the window, since sunflower seeds were Herbie's favorite food. Decades later, she still remembers the beautiful lesson her father taught her about saying goodbye.

I remember to this very day our first backyard fish funeral when our daughter, Hannah, was four. When it was her turn to talk about her fish, she said, "He was a very beautiful fish. And he was a good fish because he always ate all his food." Then, knowing full well her father's calling, she turned to me and said, "Daddy, a few words?"

However you do it, you can help children learn not to run away from death and sadness, but to face them with love.

There is a small, obscure constellation of settlements called the Bruderhof, numbering about three thousand people across four continents. In an article in *The New York Times Magazine*, writer Molly Young describes them this way:

Members are pacifists who renounce private property, live simply, dress modestly. . . . "Amish-adjacent" is probably the easiest way to describe them, but they're allowed to have smartphones, drive cars and upload (utterly delightful) You-Tube videos.

She goes on to chronicle how the Bruderhof responded to one of their own who gave birth to a stillborn baby.

The day after the couple returned, a busload of men and women from a neighboring settlement showed up to take over daily operations. For ten days this fleet of visitors cooked, cleaned and performed whatever tasks needed doing while the home community paused. "It felt like something from 'Lord of the Rings,'" my friend told me. "All of a sudden this ancillary battalion shows up over the hill, and you feel like you might win the battle."

Every culture—and every family—has its own way of mourning. Common to them all is gathering together after the burial or cremation with people who care and can help you remember. In all cases, these gatherings are meant to ease the burden on the mourners. This means we are supposed to take care of them, they are not supposed to throw a party to entertain us. When someone you care about becomes a mourner, help organize the food, the parking, the chairs—everything needed for the gathering at their home or elsewhere.

The Talmudic sages knew what they were doing when they mandated seven days and nights of being taken care of by the community, of staying home, staying put, taking the time to remember and to pray. In Hebrew this custom is referred to as *shiva*. This word literally means seven, because after arriving home from the funeral and lighting a candle that will burn for seven days, the mourners dedicate a full week to refraining from their regular activities, staying inside together, and grieving. For seven days, often sitting on low stools or pillows to physically mimic their emotional state, to literally feel "low," the mourners are surrounded and taken care of by their community of family and friends.

The entire seven days is meant to be what psychologists call a holding environment—a time and place where it is safe and accepted to grieve. There are several clearly prescribed ways for those who come to comfort the mourners to behave. Whether or not you are Jewish, these notions about how to behave around those who have lost a loved one are full of pragmatic wisdom. When you arrive at the mourners' home or wherever the gathering might be, you are not to approach the mourners. Just be close by so they can summon you if they wish. If they do, you are not to distract them by avoiding the subject of their loved one's death. In other words, don't make small talk about the news, politics, sports, or anything else. Talk about their loved one, share your memories. They want to remember. They need to remember, to talk, to let it out, to grieve.

I remember well being surrounded by cousins, friends of my parents I had not seen in decades, friends of my siblings whom I had not seen since high school—all of them there to help me and my family bear the weight and exhaustion of grief. The knowledge that they too missed my dad and had their own memories of him—memories consistent with the loyal, generous, tough, hilarious, food- and fun-loving guy I had missed so much in those first few hours after the funeral and so many hours since—pierced my sense of isolation and gave me faith that I and life and laughter would go on. I was numb after the funeral, but I still felt keenly the love of others who cared and remembered and did not want me to be alone. Shiva lifted me up when I was so down. And of course there was food, and plenty of it. It is customary to eat round foods at a shiva meal—bagels, Bundt cakes, hard-boiled eggs; reminders that we are all part of the cyclical nature of life and death. There is great wisdom in feeding mourners. The mundane act of eating is a profound affirmation that life really does go on. As I went in for my second round of smoked fish piled high on a sesame bagel and a big slice of sweet noodle kugel, I could hear my dad, as he so often said after devouring a gigantic portion of something delicious, "What little I had was good." I smiled inside. I felt . . . better. Just hours after burying my dad, life, and he, were emerging into the light.

Each morning and evening during shiva, there is a brief prayer service during which the mourners recite a prayer called the Kaddish. This prayer is always said when the dead are remembered, but the prayer itself does not contain a single reference to death. Instead, it is entirely about the greatness and the goodness of God, or the eternal spirit of the universe, or nature, or the mystery of creation, or whatever words you are comfortable with to describe the power and force behind life and death. The Kaddish must be said in a group of no fewer than ten people, assuring the mourners will not be alone during that first, difficult week, and the prayer must be said standing up. I have always understood this to be a powerful imperative. When we least feel like it, when it is hardest to affirm the greatness and goodness of life, when we are in a darkness too dark to see, with the help of friends and family we see that we can still stand, we can remember the past and step however slowly into a different future. A man whose thirty-year-old daughter died in a car accident said at the shiva as he looked around the room at the people who came to comfort him, "This changes nothing. But it means everything."

Another beautiful custom concludes the seven days of shiva, one that I have participated in many times. On the morning of the final day of hunkering down at home and being cared for by others, the rabbi and everyone gathered walk the mourners outside and around the block for the first time since returning from the cemetery. I literally, and of course metaphorically, walk the mourners back into life. As with the dying, so too for the mourners after death, showing up really matters. Hold a shiva or a wake, or some other kind of one-day gathering or whatever you can arrange even if only by Zoom, and I promise that it will hold you when you need so badly to be held.

Of course, metaphors about the long, sometimes difficult, sometimes glorious journey that is life do not really apply when a death is hard to make sense of. All deaths are sad, but some are both sad and tragic. What do we say, and more important, what do we *not* say in the face of a senseless, tragic death?

When you arrive to comfort those whose loved one has died by suicide or been killed in some sort of accident, just hold them and recall with them something beautiful about their loved one. Don't call suicide a selfish act. Don't call an overdose or accident stupid or foolish. Don't tell them you can't imagine how they feel. This is something I learned many years ago from a friend whose son died by suicide. He said there were two things that bothered him the most when people came to console him. The first was when people said, "I can't imagine what you are going through." This bothered him because he knew that, for the fellow parents at least, this wasn't true. He knew that at some point every parent envisages his or her child dying. It might be when they get their driver's license and they're not home by curfew, or it might be when you send them off to college alone, or who knows when? But every person who is a parent has imagined the worst, and pretending otherwise to someone who is living through the worst is hurtful. Instead of "I can't imagine how you are feeling," try "This is every parent's worst fear, and I am so sorry it has become a reality for you."

The other thing that bothered my friend terribly after his son died was that nearly everyone showed up at his door with sad, drawn faces. He would have preferred people just to be with him in death as they were with him in life—not to show up with overly sorrowful faces or to attempt to distract him from his grief by making small talk and pretending it was just another visit on just another day. What he needed was for his friends to be real, to be themselves with him in death as they were with him in life.

Many people feel quite awkward when they show up to comfort mourners. In those awkward moments, they often feel the need to talk, and what they say often makes the mourners feel worse, not better. Take to heart this advice from Rita Moran, a woman whose young daughter died in a car accident. I read it many years ago, and I have yet to find anything that says it better:

> *Please, don't ask me if I'm over it yet.*
> *I'll never be over it.*
> *Please, don't tell me she's in a better place.*
> *She isn't with me.*
> *Please, don't say at least she isn't suffering.*

I haven't come to terms with why she had to suffer at all.

Please, don't tell me how I feel

Unless you have lost a child.

Please, don't ask me if I feel better.

Bereavement isn't a condition that clears up.

Please, don't tell me God never gives us more than we can bear.

Please, just say you are sorry.

Please, just say you remember my child, if you do.

Please, just let me talk about my child.

Please, mention my child's name.

Please, just let me cry.

Her advice isn't about answers. It is not about why people die or about taking away the pain. She can't do that. The rabbi, minister, or therapist can't do that. Nothing but time can do that. To pretend otherwise isn't fair; it isn't fair to our grief and anguish or to our loved ones.

In "Why I Wore Black After He Died: Lessons from Victorian Mourning Culture," scholar Kari Nixon points out that in Victorian mourning culture, bodies were left in the family home long enough for families to assimilate to the new reality of a person they had always known having become a lifeless body. Black clothes were standard every day for up to two years; everything from jewelry to stationery to vehicles were marked with symbols of death. All of this served to inform the world around the mourner of his or her grief and therefore to remind others to treat that person with an added measure of sensitivity. As Nixon puts it, the black clothes and jewelry sent a mute, comforting message: "Here stands loss . . . unalterable, unutterable loss."

The Bible tells us that the wandering Israelites lived beneath a cloud sometimes. Maybe it was a cloud of confusion, maybe sadness; perhaps it was just an ordinary cloud. The Bible doesn't say. What it does say is that whether it was two days or a month or a year—however long the cloud lingered—the Israelites remained encamped. Only when it lifted did they continue on their journey toward the Promised Land. There is no magical formula given for making the cloud disappear, no incantation, no prayer, no slap on the back, no support group, no self-help book, no blind date. Just a settling in with the sadness, a sometimes slow but always sacred space for healing.

It's understandable to want to move quickly through a loss, to put the pain behind us. But the truth is that healing takes time. Rushing past pain isn't fair to our hearts. Urging others to move too quickly through their own sorrow is foolish and cruel. Through years of wandering, loss, and faith, the sages grasped what confounds so many of us when we lose a loved one, the unavoidable truth that there must be a peacemaking, a reckoning for all of us with what I like to call "God time," and that sometimes we can move forward only by staying put.

7

An Ocean of Grief

It's so curious; one can resist tears
and "behave" very well in the hardest hours of grief.
But then someone makes you a friendly sign behind a window,
or one notices that a flower that was in bud only yesterday
has suddenly blossomed, or a letter slips from a drawer . . .
and everything collapses.

—COLETTE

In a way I still knew little of death and grief until I buried my father slightly a year before beginning this book. His disease and his death revealed the powerful, disturbing, painful, beautiful lessons that only loss can teach us. I marveled at the way he accepted the diagnosis twelve Thanksgivings ago.

"Leonard," my mother said matter-of-factly, "the doctor says you have Alzheimer's."

"Really?"

"Yes, really."

"Dad, do you have any questions?" I asked.

"Nope. I know you kids love me and will do your best to take care of me. It is what it is."

Then he yawned (exhausted each day by noon from the hard work that thinking had already become), lay down on the couch in my sister's basement, and took a nap. Facing the facts without drama or remorse was classic Dad.

Dad was strong. Ten damn years with Alzheimer's—amazing what you can get used to. At first we got used to him trying to make phone calls with the TV remote. Then there were the car accidents, the confusion, the extra time it took him to pay the bills at the office, the way he could no longer find things or figure out an 18 percent tip, his angry outbursts, his withdrawal. We watched it all as if in slow motion.

He was right about our doing our best to take care of him. Even Mom, who mostly struggled with him through fifty-five years of a terrible marriage before the diagnosis, tried hard for a while—dressing him in the morning like her eleventh grandchild. She kept him at home until one night he fell in the bathroom with the door locked, stuck there trapped and urine soaked until morning. The paramedics took him to the hospital and he never came home again.

The new normal was a nursing home, where Dad seemed to enjoy the aquarium and singing along to "You Are My

Sunshine." His singing that song to the five of us kids in the back of the station wagon was one of the few joyful things I remember about my father when I was young. "You'll never know, dear, / How much I love you. / Please don't take my sunshine away." Somehow I knew he meant it. He really loved us. Years later, watching the well-meaning nursing home volunteer with her guitar coax those words from my father's failing brain broke my heart.

There would be plenty more heartbreak where that came from—seeing him in a diaper and bib for the first time; watching him being hoisted from his wheelchair to his bed with a lift, dangling and helpless like a marionette. The catheter, the baby food, the drool. Like most boys, I watched my dad shave in the morning with awe. Never did I think I would be shaving him while he stared blankly into space.

Despite his lack of formal education, my father was a natural professor of sorts; he was always teaching. Usually, each lesson included a Yiddishism from his childhood. If the day's topic was "Things could always be worse," he quipped. "*Iz beser vie a geshfir aoyf deyn hinter*"—It's better than a boil on your ass. No matter how anxious, sad, frightened, or defeated we felt, no matter what terrible things we thought we were facing in our teenage angst, the idea of its being better than a boil on our ass always made us laugh.

But Dad was right. A boil on your behind is no joke. At

the time that expression was coined, there were no antibiotics. A bedsore meant almost certain death from infection. Six months after he entered the first nursing home, my mom called to say she was moving him to a new home because the care was awful and he had a bedsore on his butt. I wept.

In the quiet of endless days my tough, frightening, crude, funny, and wickedly smart dad slipped mostly away. His memory and body were nearly gone; he sat in his nursing home wheelchair and stared blankly, asleep most of the time. Often he did not know my name. Every day the disease gained ground. Eventually it won. But it also lost. Alzheimer's lost when it tried to fracture my family. We group-chatted and talked and visited with one another, in some ways closer than ever before. Alzheimer's lost when it tried to distance me from my dad, teaching me instead how much it meant just to sit in silence and hold his hand until he fell asleep.

I think again about shaving him in his wheelchair, feeling both heartbroken and deeply moved by the intimacy of it all—touched by his tender dependency on me in that moment. Of course, the world was safer when my dad could protect me. My mind flashes back to when I was very young, maybe eight or nine, and my dad, for the first time I can recall, took my brother and me on a three-day fishing trip to a lake lodge in Minnesota. I doubt my father or my brother remembered the incident, but it is embedded in me. One night we heard something scurrying around the cabin, and it scared me. I remember my dad saying it was just a mouse and, "Let's find the little guy and give him something to eat," while putting a piece of bread on the floor. "He's just a little guy who's hungry." I don't remember what happened next, but I do remember feeling safe because my dad was there, turning something that loomed large in my childhood psyche into "just a little guy who's hungry." How could I now be shaving my once-strong dad? The old Yiddish proverb is true: "When a father gives to his son, both laugh; when a son gives to his father, both cry."

In a way, Alzheimer's weaned me from my dad and started me grieving that loss long before he actually died. People with diseases that involve memory loss really do die twice. But still, there is a shocking finality, a heavier grief, when death finally comes. That journey began when my mother called and simply said, "Steven, your father died an hour ago."

Grief is surprising. Not at first, when you are prepared for it to pick you up and slam you against the rocky shore, but later, in a month or two or ten. Anyone who thinks the shortest distance between two points is a straight line does not understand grief.

I am fine, I am out to dinner with friends and casually take a crust of bread to soak up the last drops of sauce—wiping my plate spotlessly clean. *Hmmm, just like my dad,* I think while Betsy and our friends keep chattering. *He would have loved this sauce, this bread.* I am fine. I want to cry. I am fine. I want to cry. "I really miss my dad," I say to Betsy, fighting back tears. She nods. She knows. Her dad is dead too. I want to go home. Instead, I push it all down.

I realize in that moment I need to protect myself more than I have. Returning too quickly to public life is typical of me, but such an act is not my friend. The sages of the Talmud set up an elaborate set of rules for mourners, carefully defining the dos and don'ts for the entire first year. They knew that the first birthday, the first year's worth of holidays, the first wedding anniversary, the first year of nothing but firsts, needed to be structured in a way that helped protect the mourner, at least a little, from having to face too much too soon. The first three days of grief are called "days of weeping," and during those first difficult days, we are given the space and time to just . . . cry. The first seven days are the time for shiva, when we hunker down as a family in our home and allow our community of friends to surround us and take care of us. We do not engage with the outer world. Then when those seven days are over, we reemerge into our work, school, and "normal" lives except we continue to say the Mourner's Prayer each morning, afternoon, and evening for thirty days following the funeral; we also continue to avoid celebrations and entertainment. In the special case of a parent's dying, the children say the prayer three times a day for eleven months and continue to avoid parties, concerts, and other forms of public entertainment.

All of these guidelines are intended to give mourners the physical and spiritual space to attend to our suffering. This is a beautiful example of how we can create by ceasing to do certain things. Another way of explaining this concept to those who are grieving is the simple fact that behind every no is a yes. This is particularly important for people to remember during times like weddings and the holidays, when the pain of loss is heightened by the empty chair at the table or by being surrounded by happy, celebrating people when you are feeling so low. When someone you love has died and that first set of holidays approach, there are ways to protect yourself, and you should.

Behind every no is a yes, and the holidays are an opportunity to say no to protect your own vulnerability and your own sensitive soul. When you are grieving, saying no to others may be saying yes to yourself. Say no to big parties and all that booze and all those calories in favor of time spent with your closest friend or dearest family member with whom you can talk about your loved one, your memories, your loss. Say no to the shopping and say yes to a charity that needs the money more than the department store. Say no to the people you do not want to see because they push your buttons, even if that's family, and say yes to being with the few who matter. Say no to the noise outside and yes to being home under a blanket by a fire with a good book. Say, "No, I cannot be happy this year because my heart is aching. But I can be good and gentle and kind, especially to myself."

We lose so much to death. Half our memory is gone with the death of the only person on earth who shared that incredible trip, the pizza from that little place down that alley in Rome, the babies' first stumbles across the room, that old white Ford we took cross-country when we were young and had no money. We lose so much love to death, and if that love was real and deep, the grief is real and deep. Grief is not a race to be won or an illness to be cured. To deny grief its due is to deny love.

After thirty days I removed that torn black ribbon, and you could not tell by looking at me that I was in mourning. You still cannot tell by looking at me. Sometimes I wish you could. I wish people could know when I am missing my dad— like some neon sign blinking above my head that reads, "Be gentle with me. Please. I am missing my dead father so much right now, right this very moment that I am standing here in front of you. If you have buried someone you love, then you know how I feel. It hurts right now." It would encourage people to treat me with a welcome measure of kindness. But at the same time, I don't want people to know that sometimes, because grief knows no boundaries, when I am with them, I am really with my dad, far away, far within myself. We who mourn walk in a fog sometimes. We fake it a lot. We wear a mask of normalcy, and sometimes you are talking to that mask, not us. We may be elsewhere because of our grief. That is the truth that we want you to know and the truth we also hide.

The fact that my father's burial was the morning of the eve of Yom Kippur, that holiest of days, meant that there was no shiva for him. A holy day ends shiva even if it has not been observed for all seven days, or for a single day. It was just like my dad to be buried on a day that prevented us from any, as he would have put it, *mishigas*—the perfect Yiddish word for craziness, nonsense. This meant that as soon as Yom Kippur was over, I was on a plane back to Los Angeles and back to work. The son had to once again become the rabbi, when only two days before, the rabbi was a son. I wish I could say that all my years as a rabbi prepared me in some way to handle my grief better than others do. But it isn't true. When it comes to missing my dad, I am entirely his son.

Prayer helps. The sages knew what they were doing when they commanded me to say the mourner's Kaddish three times a day for eleven months. I said it every morning for my dad and then spent a moment looking at one of my favorite pictures of him—one with his arm around me, smiling. The picture was taken before the diagnosis and the dementia, when he knew who I was and knew he loved me and knew I loved him; and he did not know that his brain would die a slow and terrible death of which he would be mostly and strangely unaware.

"Where are you, Dad?" I wondered each time I visited him in the nursing home as he stared silently into the distance. "Where are you, Dad?" I wept so many times in that elevator on the way down from his floor. Shuddering a little, doing my best to finish crying and wipe my face before the doors opened into the lobby.

Many days Kaddish—those words that we are commanded to say, those words that we do not want to say—was the only thing that helped me. When we are sad and see mostly darkness within, when we are bent low, Kaddish commands us to stand up anyway, to stand up and say, "Magnified and sanctified may His great name be in the world that He created as He wills." "As *He* wills," not you.

You are so sad, Steve, but now you must stand up and affirm and remember and say out loud how glorious life is. The world pulses with life, your father loved life, you love life. Affirm that now, even though you are bowed with grief; stand up and affirm the greatness and the goodness and the supreme power of God, who determined long ago that neither you nor anyone can conquer death, so you should strive to really live while you are alive. "Magnified and sanctified may His great name be." I was rescued so many mornings by those words, that truth that must be said out loud and standing whether I felt like it or not, whether in that moment I believed it or not.

I don't know how people get through grief without some ritual to remember, some vessel into which you can pour your sadness so that it is contained for the rest of the day, or at least enough to function. For me, it was saying Kaddish, but it could also be lighting a candle each day or gazing at a picture or reciting the Twenty-Third Psalm or some other prayer or poem, or holding or wearing some object that belonged to your loved one. The Victorians created jewelry with hair from their deceased loved ones woven into it. Find something, anything that works as permission to remember, to be sad and then to say, now, I can go on, at least for today.

Reaching out helps. I am on sabbatical holed up in my sister's empty house in Palm Springs for the entire month of May trying to write the first draft of this book. For hours each day, I think of nothing but death. I keep the house cold and dark. I write and I pace each day for ten hours until it is cool enough outside to take a walk and find some dinner. Most nights I walk around the golf course where I walked with my dad a thousand times over all the years I visited him and Mom at their Palm Springs condo just off Highway 111. As I walk, I wonder out loud, "Where are you, Dad? Where are you?" I look up, and there on the back patio of a golf course condo I see a sign containing the lyrics to "You Are My Sunshine."

I text my three sisters and my brother a picture of the sign. "Walking Mesquite golf course missing Dad so much and saw this sign." Sherry texts back a sketch of Dad: "I couldn't sleep last night and drew this." Greg texts back the lyrics to Dad's favorite Hank Williams song:

> *The silence of a falling star*
> *Lights up a purple sky*
> *And as I wonder where you are*
> *I'm so lonesome I could cry*

"You guys are all making me cry now," Marilyn responds. Somehow knowing they miss Dad as well helps me. It means I am not alone. I am not the only one who loved him or who remembers him or who cares about him and is grateful to him and yet must accept the decree. Do not dwell alone in your grief. Reaching out really can help us heal.

Helping others helps. Here's a true story (from *A Treasury of Comfort* by Sidney Greenberg) about a miracle witnessed by a clerk in a cemetery office.

Every week for several years, the mild little man received a money order and a note from a woman instructing him to put fresh flowers on her son's grave. Then one day he met her face-to-face. A car drove up to the cemetery gates and a chauffeur came into the clerk's office to speak to him. "The lady outside is too ill to walk," he explained. "Would you mind coming with me to speak with her?"

The shy clerk walked over and looked into the car, where a frail, elderly woman with sad eyes sat in the back seat. A great bundle of flowers was in her arms. "I am Mrs. Adams. Every week for years I've been sending you a money order."

"For the flowers!" the clerk exclaimed. "I've never failed to place them on your son's grave."

"I came here today myself because the doctors have told me I have only a few weeks left. I'm not sorry really. I have nothing left to live for. But before I die, I wanted to take one last look at my son's grave and to put the flowers there myself."

"You know, ma'am, I was always sorry you kept sending the money for the flowers."

"Sorry?"

"Yes. Because the flowers last such a short time, and no one ever gets to see them or smell them. You know, there are thousands of people in hospitals and nursing homes that love flowers, and they can see them and smell them. But there isn't anyone in that grave. Not really."

The old woman did not answer. She sat for a while and left without a word. The clerk was afraid he had offended her. But a few months later he was surprised with another visit. But this time there was no chauffeur. The woman sat at the wheel, driving herself. "I take the flowers to the people myself," she said to the clerk with a smile. "You were right; it does make them happy. And it makes me happy. The doctors don't understand what's making me well. But I do."

Tragedy and sorrow come to us all. It's part of what it means to be human and alive. So if we have one miracle to make our own, one strength to choose—let it be the ability to turn curses into blessings, to draw joy from sadness and life from death. Let it be the strength of an old woman and her flowers. Death is a great teacher if it impels us to serve the living.

The simple passing of time also helps. Irv came to see me thirteen months after we buried his wife—his partner in life for sixty years. Everything was done in our ancient way: The funeral with its torn black ribbons and clods of earth hitting plain pine. The shiva with its prayers, pleasantries, and Bundt cakes. A year of Kaddish, of saying the Mourner's Prayer three times a day, ending with an unveiled marker capturing his love for her in words as terse as haiku. It's been more than a year, but Irv tells me he doesn't want to move on. He's too sad. Misses her every day. Tried dating, couldn't stomach it. Tried the support group—full of women with more time and money than good sense. Parties? Too much happiness to stand. Sure, he loves the kids and the grandchildren, the Sunday dinners, and tennis four days a week. But he aches.

What should I say to Irv, who sat on the lumpy old couch in my office, looking lumpy and old himself, asking me why he cannot shed his darkness? "My friends and my children say that I should move on," he tells me, fighting back the tears. "But I don't want to move on. Am I . . . normal?" he asks after a long pause.

So I talk to Irv about time. Not the time of clocks and calendars, but the realm of time that cannot be accelerated, despite our attempts to smoke, drink, spend, or work around it. The time it takes to heal, breathe, laugh again, and move on. The pace of human existence governed by what I call *God time*. I tell Irv about my friend Barry, who discovered the pace of God time after his brother died by suicide. At first Barry tried to rush his grief but found he could only suffer. Finally he resigned himself to a lengthy stay in sorrow's home. He made peace with his sadness, took his time, learned to live in darkness. Next weekend, I tell Irv, Barry will stand beneath the white chuppah with a woman who loves him as deeply as he once hurt. It was time for the cloud to lift, just—time.

Many years ago, I read a book written by two women, both of whom had suffered the death of a child. In it, they shared what helped and what didn't. What stuck with me was their statement that the most honest and helpful thing to say to someone whose child dies is "It won't always hurt so much." I used to think that what they meant was that eventually grief abates; the ache diminishes. Now what I think they meant was not that it won't always hurt so much, but that it won't always hurt so often. It will always hurt this much when we miss our loved ones. Since my father's death and my own grief, I am through telling people it won't always hurt so much. Now I can only promise that it won't always hurt so often. That is the truth. The other is a lie.

You want to remember all the time, and you want to forget. He is all you want to think about, but you do not want to think about him at all. That is the secret truth of memory in grief; it is exquisite, and it hurts.

Often, when a person dies, the doctor will say, "His heart has stopped." In the case you are about to read, this was literally not true. And for all of us who lose someone we love, the doctor is metaphorically wrong every time. Love doesn't stop. This is a story by Peter Rowe about a heart transplant, from *The San Diego Union-Tribune*:

> *A singer, songwriter and guitarist, David Ponder knows the importance of a strong, steady beat. But this was ridiculous.*
>
> *"My heart now, it's so strong," said Ponder, 60, a Poway resident who in August 2016 underwent a successful heart transplant at Sharp Memorial Hospital. "The first night home, it was beating so hard it woke me up."*
>
> *This Christmas, David Ponder is dazzled by the gifts he's received from strangers: a life-sustaining organ and a life-enhancing relationship. He's alive because a car wreck killed a man he'd never met, Coronado's Juan Carlos Lopez, 26. When surgeons removed Lopez's heart and transplanted it in Ponder's chest, two families were stitched together in sorrow and joy.*

Months after the surgery, Ponder visited Lopez's mother. The bond was instant.

"Both of us were crying and crying and crying, hugging each other," said Graciela Elliott, Lopez's mother. "After that, I listened to his heartbeat."

In life, Juan Carlos Lopez was a doting father and co-owner of a landscaping company. As Elliott reminded Ponder between his sets at House of Blues last weekend, Lopez was a vibrant personality with numerous passions.

"When I listen to David's music, I can't help but be happy," she said. "My son loved music when he was alive."

. . . On Sunday, July 31, 2016, Graciela Elliott was in church when her phone rang. Her husband, James Elliott, was calling to say that her son was in a hospital, near death.

Juan Carlos had been driving home from his cousins' house early that Sunday morning, when he fell asleep and crashed into a tree. He died Aug. 1, a month short of his 27th birthday, leaving behind a 4-year-old daughter, Vida Mía, and the landscaping business he had just opened.

"He had two jobs already scheduled," his mother said. "He was so proud."

While renewing his driver's license, Juan Carlos had agreed to be an organ donor. The accident destroyed his pancreas, but doctors were able to harvest the man's heart, liver, kidney, tissue and other organs. Graciela, herself an organ donor, took comfort in the fact that her son's death may have saved several lives. In her sorrow, this mother kept coming back to a nagging question.

"I wanted to know who had his heart," she said.

Ponder had his first heart attack at 39. Heart disease has killed generations of Ponders, so the resulting quadruple by-pass surgery seemed more of a delaying action than a cure.

He resumed performing—an Eagles tribute band here, playing behind Ricky Skaggs there—but he was living on borrowed time. Six years ago, his doctor ordered him to stop working and go on disability.

In 2014, when he and his wife moved to San Diego County, Ponder hoped to revive his career. First, though, he needed an aortic valve replacement. In April 2016, he wheeled into a Sharp Memorial operating room and was sedated.

"When I woke up, I felt the same," he said.

He needed more than a new valve. He needed a new heart.

The transplant came on Aug. 5, 2016. Ponder seemed to recover quickly, leaving the hospital only two weeks after surgery, but medications and anxiety wore him down. In the first month, post-transplant, he lost 50 pounds. . . .

Another worry nagged at him. He had filled out the paperwork, asking to meet with his donor's family, but there had been no response. Most families decline this offer—"It's too hard," Ponder said—but he had hopes. When months passed in silence, he called Lifesharing, the nonprofit that supervises transplants. They had lost his letter; it had never gone to the donor's family.

A new letter reached its destination. In July 2017, David and [his wife], Jadie Ponder, pulled up outside Graciela Elliott's home in Coronado. There was a banner outside: "Welcome, David!"

. . . And it wasn't just Graciela Elliott who immediately adopted the Ponders. The dead man's little daughter, now 7, wrapped these strangers in bear hugs. Lopez's sister, meanwhile, came forward with a little surprise.

"I want you to meet my son," Amy Lopez said, holding out a month-old infant. "David Juan Carlos."

Graciela and James Elliott left town this Christmas, so the Ponders won't spend the holiday with them. They were together the previous two Christmases and celebrate birthdays, Thanksgivings and other special occasions as one surgically constructed family. Graciela, 48, always puts her ear to Ponder's chest, listening to a younger man's strong, steady beat.

It's a moving story about the power of a heart. To me, it matters little that the heart is a literal one, because I have learned in my grief and my journey since my father's death that his heart beats within me often and in ways far more beautiful than I had ever thought possible. When I am eating something delicious or walking among the boulders of the Joshua Tree National Park, or see ripe lemons on a tree and think about pocketing one, or listen to a salesman and am certain he is full of shit, or watch my son handle tools or hear my daughter look at a big steak and say, "Papa would have loved this," or when I sit down to write and use some rhetorical device I learned in college because my dad worked hard so that I could go to such a great college where I learned so much, or when I see a red flannel shirt or clunky shoes or a hot fudge sundae, or when the only expression that fits a situation perfectly is in Yiddish, or when I am afraid, or, or, or . . . If I could put my ear to my own chest, I know my father's heart still beats within.

Memory is light, illuminating and reminding me of so many things about my dad; reminding each of us who mourn a love both gone and yet still present, still warm and aglow even when skies are gray. If we remember, nothing can ever take our sunshine away.

8

Nobody Wants Your Crap

To have more does not mean to be more.
—ABRAHAM JOSHUA HESCHEL

After her mother died, I asked my friend Debra what she learned from it all. "Nobody wants your crap!" she answered. Everyone knows deep down that you really can't take it with you, but still, we live so much of our lives as if we can. We spend so much time worrying and working, working, working to buy so much that amounts to—nothing.

One day a group of tourists from America, traveling in Eastern Europe, went to visit the famous Rabbi Israel Kagan, known as the "Chofetz Chaim," in his town of Radun. When they came to see him, they saw the world-famous rabbi in a small study with a rickety desk and a few books.

One of the incredulous tourists said, "Rabbi, where is all your stuff?"

The Chofetz Chaim smiled. "Where is all yours?"

"But," the man answered, "we are just passing through."

The Chofetz Chaim nodded. "Me too."

I sat next to a woman on a plane back to Los Angeles from Cincinnati. I don't usually talk to people on planes because I have to lie about what I do in order to get any peace. In this case I was honest and said I was a rabbi. The woman immediately handed me her card. She owns a nationwide business called Everything But The House. She sells the stuff in people's homes after they die. Their children don't want it. No one they know wants it. The business grosses eight figures a year. We spend our lives acquiring things we think matter. Mostly they don't.

So what does matter? Walk through a cemetery and you can tell pretty quickly just by reading the headstones. Headstones limit you to only a few lines and a handful of characters to summarize a person's most significant accomplishments in life. Headstones are an exercise in essentialism, and that essentialism almost always comes down to the same few simple things. Loving husband, father, grandfather, brother, and friend. Loving wife, mother, grandmother, sister, and friend. Never once in the thousand or more times I have walked through cemeteries have I ever seen someone's net worth, GPA, résumé, or number of Instagram likes on a headstone. Abraham Joshua Heschel was right when he said, "The things we acquire . . . terminate abruptly at the borderline of time." My Yiddish-speaking grandmother put it another way: "A burial shroud," she quipped, "has no pockets."

I asked my firefighter friend how most people behave when their house suddenly bursts into flame. What do they grab in the panicked, smoke-filled seconds before running out the door or climbing down from the second-floor window? "People, pets, and pictures," he answered without a moment's hesitation. People and pets made perfect sense to me. But pictures winning the bronze was a surprise. What about fine jewelry, your hard drive, Grandma's china, cash, or the Picasso? What makes pictures, which are of no material value, ultimately so precious when things really heat up? Sure, some of us have taken the time to digitize all those photos in all those albums put together over all those years. But most of us, despite our best intentions, haven't really made all that much progress, and our favorite photos of our favorite people and moments from the past remain, as my millennial kids would put it, IRL (in real life). If your photos are in the cloud, they are in fact even less "real" than those in your home, and you can imagine what it would feel like if you lost them all forever in a cyberattack. They were never "real," and yet losing them would break your heart.

If you think about your own favorite photos, you can immediately grasp that pictures are priceless because they represent moments in time with the people we love. There's the one of my dad, with sparkling blue eyes and a wide smile, wearing baggy pants and a cowboy hat and eating a slice of grapefruit at a desert roadside stand. It reminds me of the way he found joy in the simplest of things and somehow always made me feel like everything was going to be okay. There's another of my mom, hovering over an enormous pot of soup with a spoon the size of a canoe paddle, carrying me back to how much warmth she brought to our home on those cold Minnesota nights. Shots of my son's freckled face bobbing in the ocean and my daughter's cornrowed, beaded hair put me with them on vacation in Mexico, feeling free and calm. That honeymoon beach pic of Betsy reminds me just how long and beautiful the road has been these past thirty-five years. Moments really are more precious than jewels. There is a sacredness to time that all the work for all the money for all the things in the world will never give us.

One of the most insightful life lessons I have ever read is the medieval philosopher Maimonides's treatise on the three reasons for human suffering in the world. The first reason is simply the nature of being human, the fact that all living things die, including us. To be made of animate matter and able to act upon nature means that our own matter will decline as nature acts upon us. This is not some capricious, unfair decree. It is just the definition of what it means to be a living being. In order to live, a being must necessarily eventually die. The only way to escape decline and death is to be an inanimate object, much like a stone. It is death every bit as much as life that makes us fully human.

The second source of suffering identified by Maimonides is the violence one human being perpetrates upon another. This evil, he points out, is rare in the sense that most people are peaceful most of the time in most places all over the world.

But the third form of evil that Maimonides points out is prevalent and damaging: the evil we do to ourselves because of excess. We want too much, we eat too much, we drink too much, we acquire too much. "For the more we desire to have that which is superfluous," he observed, "the more we meet with difficulties." The race toward excess led to terrible problems when Maimonides lived nine centuries ago, and the same is true today.

When I give talks to a room full of people about the importance of appreciating time, I often begin by asking the sex addicts to raise their hands. No one does. Then I ask the same of all the alcoholics, gambling addicts, pillheads, and potheads. Again, no hands. Next I invite all the racists, homophobes, sexists, and bigots to fess up. None ever take the bait. Despite the fact that there are many people with at least one of the above traits in the room, they do not raise their hands because at the very least they know their demon is nothing to be proud of. But then when I ask all the workaholics in the room to own up to their addiction, many shoot up their hands and laugh with a perverse sort of pride. Workaholism is the last acceptable *ism* in our society. And it is killing us.

Emails nagging us at all hours like crying babies. The phone buzzing, pinging, blinking, and ringing in the car, on the plane, on the dinner table, in the bathroom. Deal stress. Market stress. Commuting stress. We hit our sales goal, we raise the goal. We make VP, we aim for senior VP. Stress-induced irritable bowel syndrome, heart disease, obesity, diabetes, headaches, depression, and anxiety be damned. We have work to do! "How proud we often are . . . of the abundance of commodities we have been able to produce," Heschel observes. "Yet our victories have come to resemble defeats. . . . It is as if the forces we had conquered have conquered us." Heschel wrote those words in 1951. Materialism caused suffering then, and things have become even worse in the seventy years since Heschel first penned his warning.

The folly of confusing the material with the spiritual is nothing new. The Hebrew prophets, Jesus, Muhammad, and

Buddha all railed against idolatry millennia ago. They knew that mistaking our outer, material lives for an inner life was the road to a nagging sense of emptiness. Confusing net worth with self-worth, hoping the material will create something within us that is spiritual, is, as the philosopher Jacob Needleman describes it, "like trying to eat a picture of food." Maybe that was Moses's precise point when, as the Bible tells it, he ground the Golden Calf into powder, spread it upon the waters, and forced the ancient Hebrews to drink it.

Don't get me wrong, I like money as much as the next guy, and Heschel was no ascetic, either. We all have to make a living and we work plenty hard to do it. Heschel's plea, which of course is the plea of the Bible, is merely for some balance, some sanity—a truce in the war for more. That's why the first time the word *holy* is used in the Bible is unexpectedly not in relation to a thing at all—not a mountain, not a temple, not a sacred scroll. Instead, the word first appears in relation to a day. "Then God blessed the seventh day and made it holy." It is time, not object, which is holy. Working, creating, and imposing one's will upon nature six days a week is enough. Even God had to stop sacrificing time for stuff a seventh of the time or the stress was going to kill Him.

So much of what defines the holiness of that seventh day is not what one does. There are only a few "thou shalts" connected to the Sabbath, but there are many "thou shall nots"; a host of things one thoughtfully and deliberately refuses to do. Its beauty is created *via negationis*—by ceasing to create, much like the idea of a sculpture, whose power is revealed by removing everything that obscures the image within—chiseled chip by chiseled chip. Imagine a day free from cell phones, emails, social media, and crap on TV; a day on which we do not spend money, so there is no acquiring, no paying bills, no standing in line at checkout counters, no thought or power given over to our hunger for things.

We are forbidden to "kindle a fire" on the Sabbath. For our ancestors, starting a fire required great physical labor antithetical to a day of rest for the body and mind. But I have always understood this to mean we should refrain not only from arduous tasks but also from igniting fires between us and the people we love—no bickering, no gossiping, no yelling, no swearing, no sniping. Consider the peace and beauty of a day on which self-righteous indignation must wait until tomorrow. For those of us who take these prohibitions seriously, it is amazing to see and to feel the delicate beauty, grace, depth, and meaning that thrives in the absence of stress. It is time spent savoring time. A day devoted to being better, not better off. And it is amazing to see what is possible in life when we do something other than work, work, work, work, work, work.

After the workaholics in the room have raised their hands, I then ask everyone who would like an additional seven weeks of vacation each year to help reduce their stress and burnout to raise their hands. Everyone does. I remind them that there are fifty-two weeks in a year, and if we take a day each of those weeks to unplug, it amounts to seven weeks of vacation from the madness. This is simple math that will change your life.

There is a kind of super-Sabbath in the Bible called a sabbatical year; every seventh year the ancient Israelites were forbidden to work their land. That might seem like nothing more than pragmatic ecology. Farmers know that letting fields lie fallow every once in a while results in better yields later on. But there is a deep spiritual concept at work here too, when you consider that not only did land have to lie fallow during the sabbatical year, but also all private debts were suspended and all indentured servants set free.

The Hebrew word for holiness, *kedusha*, literally means removed or apart. We can achieve a real sense of holiness only if we remove ourselves from the mundane by setting limits that prevent it from encroaching on every aspect of our lives. It sounds paradoxical, but transcendence requires limits. To be honest, I have never been very good with limits, especially when it comes to my work. First of all, I am my father's son. His true religion, his salvation, was hard work, and I, his son, was raised in the temple of sweat. Second, the opportunities for a rabbi to teach, to build, to comfort, and to create are limitless, and therefore I thought my efforts must also be without limit. You might think the weekly Sabbath was a respite for me, but in truth it was just the opposite. Most of the time, the Sabbath was among the most stressful of my days: an evening and day spent on the pulpit in front of hundreds, attempting to teach scripture in a way that would resonate, fretting about my sermon, worrying about the bar or bat mitzvah kid getting it right, worrying about people being moved by the experience, stewing about getting to the hospitals in time to pay Sabbath visits to temple members and still get home in time to prepare my remarks for a wedding that night, put on another suit, and head out in traffic, hoping I won't be late.

But then in 2020, a novel coronavirus appeared, forcing all of us to rein in most aspects of our lives—our contact with one another, our travel, our socializing, our spending, and our work. It was a global pause, a cessation of so many of the ambitions and so much of the commotion and turmoil of our former lives—lives in which so many of us felt a lot like indentured servants. How paradoxical that this confinement in which we found ourselves actually set so many of us free in so many beautiful ways—free to study, meditate, pray, take a walk, make a call, bake cookies, take a long, hot bath, and above all, spend holy, sacred time with the people we love. Much like death, there is great wisdom in cessation. Without limits, it is impossible for our spirits to soar.

The coronavirus caused a lot of us to ask ourselves some

important questions. How many meetings do we really need to attend? Did we need to spend so much time away from home for so many years? Must we have so many suits, ties, shoes, purses, and outfits to wear? How much do we have to spoil the earth by driving and buying? The global fear of death woke the entire world from its slumber; it stripped a lot of nonsense from our lives, and from that stripping away, something beautiful emerged, a knowing that we were meant to be with the people we love most.

During the pandemic I found myself forgetting things a lot. Where did I leave my phone? Did we use the avocados last night or are they in the refrigerator in the garage? Did I shower yesterday, and have I been wearing these sweatpants for three days or two, and what day is it, anyway?

Despite my forgetting, I made a lot of promises I intended to keep when the whole mess is over. I am going to drive less and work from home more, I told myself. I am going to say no to a lot more social obligations I used to say yes to. I am going to buy less, save more, keep walking and doing my core strengthening so my back doesn't hurt so much, and waste less food. I am going to keep in touch more often and tell more people I love them with the ease and frequency with which those words seemed to flow from my lips during these months of isolation. I will remain grateful for little things—paper towels and the smell of warm bread, dinner out with Betsy and the kids—and big things too, like scientists, doctors and nurses, thoughtful leaders, the courage of caregivers, springtime and life itself. I will hug and hug and hug my family and friends with all my heart. But will I?

"Without forgetting, we would have no memory at all," said Oliver Hardt, who studies memory and forgetting at McGill University in Montreal. In other words, if we remembered everything, our brains would always be swamped. "Forgetting serves as a filter," Hardt said. "It filters out the stuff that the brain deems unimportant." Covid-19 has changed our lives and revealed beautiful and powerful lessons many of us have promised to hold on to. But we are going to have to fight hard to remember and live by those lessons when the pull of our former ways reasserts itself. Our coronavirus lives have been pared down, and despite the pain and death that visited so many, for most, life was paradoxically somehow more beautiful, leaving in its wake sacred promises for each of us to keep. We are going to have to fight for that beauty to remain.

Consider this now-famous story told by a ham radio operator. He writes:

A few weeks ago, I was shuffling toward the basement shack with a steaming cup of coffee, where I sat down and turned the dial up on my ham radio. I came across an older-sounding fella with a tremendous signal and a golden voice. He was telling whoever he was talking with something about a thousand marbles.

"Well, Tom," the golden-voiced man said, "sure sounds like you're busy with your job. I'm sure they pay you well, but it's a shame you have to be away from your family so much. Hard to believe a fella has to work 60 or 70 hours a week. Too bad you missed your daughter's dance recital. Let me tell you something, Tom," the golden voice continued. "It's something that has helped me keep a good perspective on my priorities. I sat down one day and did a little arithmetic. The average person lives about 75 years—some more, some less, but on average, about 75 years. Now then, I multiplied 75 times 52 and came up with 3,900, which is the number of Saturdays that the average person has in their entire lifetime.

"Now stick with me, Tom," the man said, "I'm getting to the important part. It took me until I was 55 years old to think about this in any detail, and by that time I had lived through over 2,800 Saturdays. I got to thinking that if I lived to be 75, I had only about 1,000 of them left to enjoy. So I went to a toy store and bought every single marble they had. I ended up having to visit three toy stores to round up 1,000 marbles. I took them home and put them inside of a large, clear plastic container right here in the shack next to my radio gear. Every Saturday since then, I have taken one marble out and thrown it away.

"I found that by watching the marbles diminish, I focused more on the really important things in life. There is nothing like watching your time here on earth run out to help get your priorities straight. Now, let me tell you one more thing before I sign off and take my lovely wife out for breakfast. This morning, I took the very last marble out of the container. I figure if I make it until next Saturday, then I have been given a little extra time. It was nice to meet you, Tom. I hope you spend more time with your family. This is k9nzq, over and out."

It's a story about something the sages encouraged us to do three thousand years ago. "Number our days," they remind us, "so that we may grow a heart of wisdom." It's a simple, powerful little story. But an even more powerful story is how it came into my hands. A remarkable father handed me that story after burying his eight-month-old baby, dead from a disease that afflicts only a handful of babies in the world. Together with his courageous wife, family, and friends, we lowered a tiny coffin into the silent, gaping ground. Two hours later, he handed me the story about the marbles in a jar. "Tell people, Rabbi," he said through the tears. "Tell people to take the time. Take the time for the people you love."

Must it take a baby's death to slow us down? Is a pandemic or an appointment with the oncologist the only thing left that gets our attention anymore in this world of speed? Can't we stop trying to beat the clock like game-show buffoons and remember instead that the clock beats us? Can't we stop our nervous lives a seventh of the time for something better? Death is a wake-up call to find an antidote to the inevitable indignities, cravings, and predations of our frenetic lives during which we are so terribly busy yet feel so terribly empty sometimes. Death is a powerful reminder to buy less and do more, live more, travel more, and give more instead. Create your own kind of Sabbath in your heart and your life. Spend a seventh of your life gathered around the candlelit table, then snuggle beneath the covers. Stroll, listen, think, breathe, and relish your most sacred, finite, and beautiful blessing—time. Don't wait until your whole damn house is on fire to wake up panicked one day and realize that you've squandered your time because no one, not even you, wants your crap.

I spend a lot of time with elderly people, many of whom know they are going to die soon. They are not afraid of dying, but they do have regrets. Often they will tell me about the things they wish they had done or said differently and I have learned a lot from their mistakes. They almost all wish they had worried less about material things and more about their relationships. This is one of the most beautiful lessons death comes to teach us about how to live.

I have a geeky habit now of collecting people's thoughts about how they would live their lives differently if they had the chance to live them over again. One of them is this poem variously attributed to the Argentine poet and essayist Jorge Luis Borges and to the Colombian journalist and short story writer Gabriel García Márquez. If you believe Wikipedia— and I do, in this case—it was neither man. The first known version of the poem, titled "Moments," was published as prose in 1953 in the *Reader's Digest* under the title "I'd Pick More Daisies." The poem exists in Spanish as *"Instantes,"* and in English as both "Moments" and "Instants." Whichever, it is well known and has been published and quoted in many places and distributed widely on the Internet:

If I could live again my life, in the next—I'll try to make more mistakes,
I won't try to be so perfect, I'll be more relaxed. I'll be more full than I am now.
In fact, I'll take fewer things seriously. I'll be less hygienic. I'll take more risks.

I'll take more trips. I'll watch more sunsets. I'll climb more
   mountains.
I'll swim more rivers. I'll go to more places I've never been.
I'll eat more ice cream and fewer lima beans.
I'll have more real problems and fewer imaginary ones.
I was one of those people who live prudent and prolific
   lives—each minute of his life,
Of course I had moments of joy—
but if I could go back, I'll try to have only good moments.
If you don't know—that's what life is made of, don't lose
   the now!
I was one of those who never goes anywhere without a
   thermometer,
without a hot-water bottle, and without an umbrella and
   without a parachute,
If I could live again—I will travel light. If I could live
   again—I'll try to work barefoot
at the beginning of spring till the end of autumn. I'll ride
   more carts.
I'll watch more sunrises and play with more children
—but now I am 85 and I know that I am dying.

British American journalist Christopher Hitchens described it this way in *Hitch-22*, the memoir he wrote when he
knew he was dying:

If you were offered the chance to live your own life again, would you seize the opportunity? The only real philosophical answer is automatically self-contradictory: "Only if I did not know that I was doing so." To go through the entire experience once more would be banal and Sisyphean—even if it did build muscle—whereas to wish to be young again and to have the benefit of one's learned and acquired existence is not at all to wish for a repeat performance, or a Groundhog Day. And the mind ought to, but cannot, set some limits to wish-thinking. All right, same me but with more money, a sturdier penis, slightly different parents, a briefer latency period . . . the thing is absurd. I seriously would like to know what it was to be a woman, but like blind Tiresias would also want the option of re-metamorphosing if I wished. How terrible it is that we have so many more desires than opportunities.

The great Erma Bombeck, who suffered her entire adult life with a painful chronic illness but nevertheless chose to use her talent to make people laugh, considered the question of how she would live her life differently if she could live it all over again this way:

Instead of wishing away nine months of pregnancy and complaining about the shadow over my feet, I'd have cherished every minute of it and realized that the wonderment growing inside me was to be my only chance in life to assist God in a miracle.

I would never have insisted the car windows be rolled up on a summer day because my hair had just been teased and sprayed.

I would have invited friends over to dinner even if the carpet was stained and the sofa faded.

I would have eaten popcorn in the "good" living room and worried less about the dirt when you lit the fireplace.

I would have taken the time to listen to my grandfather ramble about his youth.

I would have burnt the pink candle that was sculptured like a rose before it melted while being stored.

I would have sat cross-legged on the lawn with my children and never worried about grass stains.

I would have cried and laughed less while watching television . . . and more while watching real life.

I would have shared more of the responsibility carried by my husband which I took for granted.

I would have eaten less cottage cheese and more ice cream.

I would have gone to bed when I was sick, instead of pretending the Earth would go into a holding pattern if I weren't there for a day.

I would never have bought ANYTHING just because it was practical/wouldn't show soil/guaranteed to last a lifetime.

When my child kissed me impetuously, I would never have said, "Later. Now, go get washed up for dinner."

There would have been more I love yous . . . more I'm sorrys . . . more I'm listenings . . .

But mostly, given another shot at life, I would seize every minute of it . . . look at it and really see it . . . try it on . . . live it . . . exhaust it . . . and never give that minute back until there was nothing left of it.

Each one of these reflections contains a lot of regret—mostly for focusing on the wrong things in life instead of taking full advantage of the time we are granted to live and to love. I find these writings instructive, funny, poignant, but also sad in the sense that for many people, the realization of what went wrong comes too late to do very much about it. After all, it is impossible to change the past. We can only change the future. If we wait until we are old to recognize what matters most, there is little future left to change. What have I learned from all of those stews of stories with all those families whose loved ones are gone? What have I learned from my collection of "If I Had My Life to Live Over Again" literature? What have I learned from so much death? Simply this: to live and love fully while I am alive.

. . .

Growing up, if my siblings or I wanted to spend money on something our father thought was frivolous, which was pretty much everything, my father warned us to be happy with what we already had because *"A bissel iz a plotz"*—a little is a lot. He grew up a skinny kid on welfare. There was a reason that as an adult he reused his dental floss and tea bags. There was a reason he washed off a paper plate and let it dry for the next time. There was a reason he buried gold coins under the big tree in the backyard. He knew the worst could happen and the only protection was hard work and pennies saved. His care when he had Alzheimer's cost $150,000 a year and he toughed it out for a decade. Right again, Dad.

I went to visit Marilyn, an elderly woman in my congregation, when she was dying. She looked up at me—gaunt, spent—and said, "Rabbi, I just want to go to dinner and a movie." To Marilyn as well, a little was a lot.

In his nineties my friend Lionel told me, "When you travel, do it right. Because when you get to be my age, you'll never miss the money and you'll be glad you have the memories." Lionel died two years ago, but I will never forget him, partly because that little piece of travel advice had an effect on the son of an extremely frugal man. Those few words of advice have given me priceless memories with Betsy and the kids that I otherwise would not have had.

I spend more now, but I am more concerned with meaningful experiences than with material things. I want to enjoy my family and my life more than I ever have before. Now I know that memories will be all that matters after that call comes to Aaron and Hannah the way it came to me about my father more than two years ago. I want to live a beautiful life so that beauty is what remains within them when I am gone. We are helpless in death, but we are not helpless in life.

A little is a lot in another way too. Death is perhaps the single greatest teacher when it comes to how large the little things in life really are. What do most of us end up regretting at the end of our lives? What's on the list? Murder? No. Rape? No. Treason? No. Instead, it's the little things—a bit of gossip, a white lie, some cash on the side, a little cynicism, an insult, a touch, a display of apathy—these are the flutters of butterfly wings and you just never know how much they might end up hurting you or another person in ways you regret forever.

It's often the little things that come between us and others. A dropped email. A thank-you note that never arrived. Gossip. A lack of caring. An unkind word. A missed birthday. Listening to others whose lives have fallen apart weep on my couch of tears, I have learned how one small moral failure can lead to another and another and another. "Sin," the Talmud reminds us, "begins with acts as thin as a spider's web and becomes as thick as cart ropes."

I was twenty-seven years old when I attended my first temple board meeting and shared my plans for a new adult education program. I started with how poorly organized and meager the current offerings were and went on to explain how I was going to fix it all. After the meeting, Rochelle pulled me aside and said, "You know, whatever you criticize was created by someone else who did their best. You might think about whether or not you really need to hurt other people's feelings to get to where you want to be." I have never forgotten these two sentences, which were full of wisdom about how I could be a better person.

But if our seemingly small moral failures stacked one upon the other make all the difference in life, then the little things we do right can make all the difference in a positive way. Whoever said "Don't sweat the small stuff" did not understand how large the small stuff really looms in life.

But a little doesn't mean a lot in a place like Los Angeles. I live in a big town, fueled by big ideas, big personalities, and big numbers. Mine is not a little temple. It is an institution with big ambitions, a big mission, a big heart, and a big budget. The ironic thing is that all that bigness obscures what is really most important. When I graduated from rabbinical school, I asked the handful of my teachers I respected the most what they thought it meant to be a successful rabbi. The best answer was from my Hebrew literature professor Ezra

Spicehandler, who was not a rabbi. "A successful rabbi," he advised, "is someone who deeply affects at least three people during the course of his career." Was Professor Spicehandler just thinking small, or was he telling me to treat each person with dignity, attention, and the hope of helping to make his or her life better because of the spiritual truths I could teach? I do not know if I have deeply affected three people in my rabbinate, but I do know that I have tried, and that I might well have been a very different sort of rabbi if not for those few words from Dr. Spicehandler.

When I sit with a family to prepare for a funeral, it's the little things that matter. The pancakes your papa made on Sundays. The cage your mom helped build for your pet salamander. The way your dad showed up for you after your divorce. When I visit a hospital room, I see the flower arrangements on the windowsill and the cards proudly propped up on the nightstand. These small gestures pierce the dark isolation of illness; they really matter. Each time someone has reached out to me to say, "I care," to say, "Thank you," to gently help me be a better person—these small kindnesses and corrections loom very large in my heart.

Grieving for my father has revealed again and again the power of the seemingly small. It means so much now to remember, to remember everything I can—every lesson, every joke and gesture. Alzheimer's was a powerful lesson in essentialism, a stripping away, leaving behind memories of the sweet man that was always at Dad's core, whose kind eyes, even at the very end, lit up when someone, anyone, said, "Hello."

In a world where we all want so much, I learned minimal expectations were best. Toward the end when I visited the nursing home, I was grateful if my father was simply awake; the smallest of things. The last time I arrived in Minneapolis from Los Angeles to visit just for the day, it had been months since he had said anything to anyone. When it was time to say goodbye, I looked at him, memorizing his blue eyes in case I never saw him alive again, and simply said, "I love you, Dad."

He stared back expressionless, pursed his lips again and again, then whispered, "And I love you too." Five words.

That turned out to be the last time I saw him alive. Now I hold on to those five words with all my might. Right again, Dad—a little really is a lot.

Deathbed goodbyes are something rabbis see a lot of, but most families experience them only once or twice if they're lucky. Our loved ones sometimes die without a chance for us to snuggle up and hold on to them as we speak our last words together. As surreal and sad as it is, there's something beautiful about a last kiss on the forehead of the ones who brought us into life, something deeply sacred about those final, whispered words.

Words seem quintessentially material and real to me. Christopher Hitchens discovered this when he battled esophageal cancer. In his book *Mortality,* he puts it this way: "I had just returned from giving a couple of speeches in California, where with the help of morphine and adrenaline I could still successfully 'project' my utterances, when I made an attempt to hail a taxi outside my home—and nothing happened. I stood, frozen, like a silly cat that had abruptly lost its meow."

Like health itself, the loss of one's voice can't be imagined until it occurs. Deprivation of the ability to speak is like an attack of impotence, or the amputation of a part of the personality. As Hitchens says:

> *In the medical literature, the vocal "cord" is a mere "fold," a piece of gristle that strives to reach out and touch its twin, thus producing the possibility of sound effects. But I feel that there must be a deep relationship with the word "chord": the resonant vibration that can stir memory, produce music, evoke love, bring tears, move crowds to pity and mobs to passion. We may not be, as we used to boast, the only animals capable of speech. But we are the only ones who can deploy vocal communication for sheer pleasure and recreation, combining it*

with our two other boasts of reason and humor to produce higher syntheses. To lose this ability is to be deprived of an entire range of faculty; it is assuredly to die more than a little.

"And what do I want back?" wrote Hitchens shortly before he died. "In the most beautiful apposition of two of the simplest words in our language: the freedom of speech."

I can remember things people said to me more than five decades ago when I was a small child. I can also recall lyrics to a song I heard half a century ago, but cannot recall what I had for breakfast two days ago. A lot of people have some sort of estate plan or at the very least a will. In that way, we are prepared for death when it comes to what will happen to our material possessions and wealth. But in the deepest sense, who gets our stuff when we die is the least important of all our bequests to the people we care most about. What matters most is the nonmaterial—the ethical, spiritual legacy of love we leave behind for our loved ones. Consider therefore the idea of creating an ethical will, a document that tells the people you love about the ideals you are leaving for them, not just the money and the jewelry.

This tradition reaches all the way back to the Bible in the deathbed scene with Jacob and his sons. Jacob has had his share of sorrow in life. He cheated his older brother Esau out of his birthright blessing. Jacob was in turn deceived and cheated by his father-in-law. Jacob's own sons lie to him and break his heart, telling him that their half brother Joseph is dead, when in fact they had sold him into slavery. Jacob's daughter Dina is raped, and as a final insult, he has to send his children away to beg the mighty pharaoh of Egypt for food. Jacob's was not an easy life. But somehow he managed to raise children in whose hands the destiny of an entire people would be placed.

Now Jacob is dying. His eyes have grown milky white and dim. He manages a final whispered statement into each of his sons' ears. Jacob tells each of them about their own character and future. He calls Reuben unstable and disgraceful. He warns Simeon and Levi about their tempers and implores them to curse their own anger. "Serve others with humility and you will be blessed," he assures Issachar. "Remember that it is God who is truly mighty," he tells the powerful Joseph. Of Judah, Jacob is proud, wishing him good fortune. In some cases, Jacob is harsh with his children, in others kind—but he is always honest. It is, after all, his last chance to guide his boys through life. These are, as the cliché goes, Jacob's final words.

Formal ethical wills date back to eleventh-century Germany, France, and Spain. There are volumes of them collected in libraries and online. We spend a lot of time accumulating wealth and possessions to leave behind for our children, hoping the material will somehow express to them the emotional. But why not leave our children and other loved ones a written account of our hopes and affection for them? For those who do not have children, ask yourself who in your life matters most and what do you want them to remember about you when you are gone. Tell them in your ethical will. I have written mine. It's a work in progress because, as is true of all of us, my life is a work in progress. To quote one of my favorite poems by Rabbi Alvin Fine:

Birth is a beginning and death a destination;
But life is a journey.
A going, a growing from stage to stage:
From childhood to maturity and youth to old age;
From innocence to awareness and ignorance to knowing;
From foolishness to discretion and then perhaps, to wisdom.
From weakness to strength or strength to weakness and often
    back again.
From health to sickness and back, we pray, to health again;
From offense to forgiveness, from loneliness to love
From joy to gratitude, from pain to compassion
From grief to understanding, from fear to faith;
From defeat to defeat to defeat, until, looking backward or
    ahead:
We see that victory lies not at some high place along the way,

But in having made the journey, stage by stage, a sacred pilgrimage. . . .

So yes, my ethical will is likely to change as I change, but I offer my current version to you now as a humble example:

Dear Aaron and Hannah,

The finest moments of my life have been with you and Mommy, sitting around our kitchen table, laughing. I never feel richer or more at peace with the world than in those moments. That kind of love is more important than anything. Spend your life with a person as good as Mommy and you will have many of those moments. And don't worry, you will know in your heart when that person arrives. It is a powerful, healing, beautiful kind of love. Grasp it.

Have a healthy relationship with work. Do your best at it, but your work is not the same thing as your life. I often confused the two and hope you will less so. Spend time in nature. It will remind you of God, of true greatness; it will calm you, cause you to pause, breathe, stand still, listen. It will help you feel humble and small in profound and important ways. Think of me when you are out there; feel and know that my soul is with you.

Do not roll your eyes at religion. Celebrate what makes you different. There is much to learn—much—from our ancestors, from prayer, the Sabbath, candles, warm bread and wine, generosity and faith while gathered around a table with people you love.

When you worry, remember that most things turn out better than we expect. When anxiety, sorrow, loss, and pain come, lean on the people you love. Do not suffer alone; it is much worse that way. This is another reason you should look for someone like Mommy to love. I would not have been able to breathe without her.

I used to love to dance, but when I became a more public person, I stopped dancing at weddings and parties. I allowed my fear of what others might think of me, fear of being a spectacle, to keep me from dancing. I regret that now. It was a bad example to you and robbed me of joy. Don't let fear of what others might think keep you from dancing or singing or loving. Let nothing and no one suppress what your soul longs for. Live so that you do not die with a longing soul.

Count your blessings. When you are feeling less than, or want more, or are mired in self-pity, which happens to us all, look around and count your blessings again and again and again until you tally a hundred of them. Everything is easier when you are grateful.

Feel for others. People behave badly because they are damaged. Let your first impulse be one of empathy. That being said, there will be a handful of people in your life who demand too much—who are mean, narcissistic, negative—causing you to feel terrible about yourself. Cut these people out of your life. You cannot fix them.

Be good and the rest works out. See the world with the people you love. Cherish time; it matters so much more than things. Mine with you and Mommy has made my life worth living. I wish for you that kind of love now. I wish for you that kind of love when I am gone. Say Kaddish and light a candle for me when I am gone. Feel its warmth and know I love you still.

Dad

Your ideals and your words will mean more than anything else you leave your loved ones. Use this ethical will as a starting place, use someone else's, or make up one completely on your own—but write one. Because the day will come for each of us when we will speak no more forever. An ethical will is our chance to articulate the beauty we want to be certain remains.

9

The Afterlife of Memory

*"Sometimes," he sighed, "I think the things I remember
are more real than the things I see."*

—ARTHUR GOLDEN,
MEMOIRS OF A GEISHA

"Close your eyes," I said to the congregation of two thousand people seated in the quiet beauty of the sanctuary. It was the holiest day of the year during a service devoted to remembering loved ones who have died.

Close your eyes and breathe in deeply.
Breathe out and relax.
Breathe in deeply again.
Breathe in peace.
Breathe in quiet.

Now place yourself in a comfortable room in your home or wherever you choose and invite into that room a loved one who has died. Bring him to life again in your mind. Bring her to life again in your mind—in your memory.

See her. See her skin, her hair.
Feel his whiskers against your cheek.
See his smile and his eyes.
Be with her.
Speak to her.
Tell her what you wish for her.
Give her your blessing.
Now allow her to leave the room.
Be with him.
Speak to him.
Tell him what you wish for him.
Give him your blessing.
Now allow him to leave the room.
Breathe deeply—and when you are ready, open your eyes.

Halfway through this visualization, the room was awash in tears, hundreds of grown men and women, weeping, longing . . . remembering. To remember is the quintessential act of being human. Not in the instinctual, mindless way of salmon swimming upstream to spawn or squirrels finding their long-buried acorns, but to use memory in a way that summons the past into the present and brings the dead back to life—willfully, specifically, tearfully, joyfully, meaningfully.

Many years ago, a woman came to see me with her son. She was old even then, in her mid-eighties for sure. Her deep-set eyes were darkly circled. She was a study in calm, with a sadness to her, the look of someone slightly lost in dementia and left behind by time. Sophia was a retired music teacher who had taught Sunday school at the temple in the 1950s. She wanted to talk about what would happen after she died. She wanted me to meet her son.

Who would preside over the funeral? How could she be certain things would be as she wanted them? She knew the previous senior rabbi, but he'd been gone for twenty-five years. She wanted me to know about her, her family, her son, her love of music. And she wanted to give something to the temple. Actually, she wanted to give everything to the temple. That afternoon Sophia told me that she was leaving everything—her house, her money—to the temple after she and her son had both died. Her son told me that he too was leaving everything to the temple. "And we are leaving the temple this violin," Sophia said to me, "with one condition." She stared into my eyes, expecting a promise of trust and care. The condition? That it be displayed in a glass case somewhere at the temple.

It was an 1840 violin by Giuseppe Sgarbi. He worked in

Finale Emilia from 1840 to 1878, and then moved to Rome. Sgarbi's son and pupil, Antonio, took over his workshop in Rome in 1890 when Sgarbi returned to Finale Emilia. Sgarbi's violins are distinguished by a personal style expressed fully through the modeling of the scrolls and his choice of wood. The best samples are covered in a shiny transparent rich orange-red varnish. It seemed a simple enough promise to keep. Yes, I promised Sophia, I would be sure that her funeral was done as she requested, and I would be sure that we displayed the violin. I thanked her and her son for their generosity to the temple, leaving her home, their money, and Sgarbi's violin in our hands, and I promised them I would keep my word.

Years passed. Dementia set deeply into Sophia's aged brain. Her son was stricken with cancer and died before she did. I went to tell Sophia the sad news. She was now alone with her caretaker. Sophia died not long after I told her about her son. And I kept every promise to her except one, because I know she would have wanted me to break it.

"A woman died and left everything to the temple," I mentioned at one of our clergy meetings soon after Sophia's death. "Her home, her money, and a violin," I added. "Where should we display the violin?"

"You can't just display a violin," one of the other rabbis said. "If you don't play it, it will die. The varnish, the wood, the tone will be ruined, gone. Violins die if you don't play them."

He was right. My research led me to an article by Ian Fisher in *The New York Times* about Cremona, Italy, and a man named Andrea Mosconi.

A violin, it turns out, needs to be played, just as a car needs to be driven. . . . In this city that produced the best violins ever made, that job belongs to Andrea Mosconi. He is 75, and for the past 30 years, six days a week, he has finger-fed 300-year-old violins, worth millions, a diet of Bach, Tchaikovsky and Bartok . . .

Every morning, Mr. Mosconi, the city's official musical conservationist, stands before pristine, multilocked glass cases and faces three violins by the Amatis (one of the first makers of the modern violin, from the mid-16th century), two by the Guarneris and four instruments—three violins and a cello—by Stradivari. Mr. Mosconi has no favorite: The very question is a mild affront.

Getting down to work, he unlocks the cases and carefully removes each instrument. He tunes them, then plays each for six or seven minutes. He starts with scales and arpeggios, then something more substantial, on a recent day part of one of Bach's partitas for the violin. Nothing less would do.

"A great instrument should get great music and also a great performer," he said. A multimillion-dollar violin in hand, he paused for a moment to ponder his own place. "Not that I am a great performer," he said. "But I do my work."

Most violinists never get near a Stradivarius and still, three decades after he began, he feels the weight of caring so closely for so many.

The weight of caring. That's what we bear when death comes to our loved ones. The weight of caring for those we love who have died but not left us and will not leave us, so long as we remember and live the lessons of their lives. I kept my promise to Sophia. Yes, we display the violin. But we do not just keep it locked behind glass; we also play it at special moments throughout the year and especially during our annual memorial service for people who have suffered a loss in the past year.

We too, we mere humans, must also actively remember our loved ones, or they too will surely die not once, as all things must, but a second, more permanent death. "The Kaddish [memorial prayer] I now say for my father, he said for his; and so back through a recession of the generations that exceeds what my imagination can grasp. . . ." wrote Milton Himmelfarb during his year of mourning. "Whatever its efficacy may be for the dead, it binds *me* up in the bundle of life, situates *me* in the procession of the generations, frees *me* from the prison of now and here. . . . To think of my father, to recall him, is to hold off his mortality—and because ritual is eloquent, to hold it off still one generation further. Where has Daddy gone? To shul [the synagogue], to say Kaddish for Grandpa."

People do not really die when the heart stops beating. As long as their lives, their values, the melody to which they lived and danced continue to play in the memories of loved ones and through their effects on the world, they live on. In her book *Tiny Beautiful Things*, Cheryl Strayed describes how her mother lives on for her.

> *The summer I was eighteen, I was driving down a country road with my mother. . . . [We] came upon a yard sale at a big house where a very old woman lived alone, her husband dead, her kids grown and gone. . . .*
>
> *We were the only people there. Even the old woman whose sale it was didn't come out of the house, only waving to us from a window. It was August, the last stretch of time I would live with my mother. . . .*
>
> *There was nothing much of interest at the yard sale . . . but as I turned away, just as I was about to suggest that we should go, something caught my eye.*
>
> *It was a red velvet dress trimmed with white lace, fit for a toddler.*

"Look at this," I said and held it up to my mother, who said, Oh, isn't that the sweetest thing, and I agreed and then set the dress back down.

In a month I'd be nineteen. In a year I'd be married. In three years I'd be standing in a meadow not far from that old woman's yard holding the ashes of my mother's body in my palms. I was pretty certain at that moment that I would never be a mother myself. Children were cute, but ultimately annoying, I thought then. I wanted more out of life.

And yet, ridiculously, inexplicably, on that day the month before I turned nineteen, as my mother and I poked among the detritus of someone else's life, I kept returning to that red velvet dress fit for a toddler. I don't know why. I cannot explain it even now except to say something about it called powerfully to me. I wanted that dress. I tried to talk myself out of wanting it as I smoothed my hands over the velvet. There was a small square of masking tape near its collar that said $1.

"You want that dress?" my mother asked, glancing up nonchalantly from her own perusals.

"Why would I want it?" I snapped, perturbed with myself more than her.

"For someday," said my mother.

"But I'm not even going to have kids," I argued.

"You can put it in a box," she replied. "Then you'll have it, no matter what you do."

194

"I don't have a dollar," I said with finality.

"I do," my mother said and reached for the dress.

I put it in a box, in a cedar chest that belonged to my mother. I dragged it with me all the way along the scorching trail of my twenties and into my thirties. I had a son and then a daughter. The red dress was a secret only known by me, buried for years among my mother's best things. When I finally un-earthed it and held it again it was like being slapped and kissed at the same time, like the volume being turned way up and also way down. The two things that were true about its existence had an opposite effect and were yet the same single fact:

My mother bought a dress for the granddaughter she'll never know.

My mother bought a dress for the granddaughter she'll never know.

How beautiful. How ugly.

How little. How big.

How painful. How sweet. . . .

But seeing my daughter in that red dress on the second Christmas of her life gave me something beyond words. . . .

My daughter is wearing a dress that her grandmother bought for her at a yard sale.

My daughter is wearing a dress that her grandmother bought for her at a yard sale.

It's so simple it breaks my heart.

We miss them. Oh, how we miss them. The phone calls. The chair that now sits empty at the table for Thanksgiving. Knowing they were there. Knowing they loved us. Letting them know we loved them. We ache. But those who are gone—our parents, grandparents, brothers and sisters, husbands and wives, friends and family—are only truly gone if we fail to live as they in their finest moments sought to live. They are only truly gone if we fail to remember—the wisdom of their old age; the times they cared for us, protected us, cheered us on, picked us up, kissed and hugged and believed in us; the moments they made us laugh, made us think, held us. To remember them—their laughter, their eyes, when they were young and handsome, beautiful and full of life—to live and play the melody they bequeathed to us, softens the pain; we embrace them in death as lovingly as they embraced us in life.

Was she kind? Then let us be kinder. Was he strong? Let us be stronger. Was she generous? Let us give more. Was he forgiving? Then let us forgive. Was she courageous? Let us find courage and be not afraid. Did he love laughter? Then let's lighten up. Did she reach out to help? Do we? If death gives meaning and purpose to life, which of course it does, then the expression of that meaning is crystallized in a simple yet profound idea. We should live our lives as good ancestors.

How are you doing at being good ancestors to the people

you love most and the ones they will love most whom you will never know? The son of a junkman, I became a rabbi and wear my father's prayer shawl on the holiest day of the year. It is so simple; it breaks my heart wide open.

When I talk to groups about the concept of being a good ancestor, I use two props. The first is a bottle of beer brewed with water from a melting glacier. Breweries are paying fishermen to go out and net the huge chunks of polar ice that are calving off glaciers due to global warming. It's the best water for brewing beer—frozen, pristine, and pure for millions of years. The second prop is a bottle of detergent manufactured by a company called Seventh Generation. The soap is environmentally friendly, and the company derives its name from a statement in the Great Law of the Iroquois Confederacy. "In our every deliberation," say the Iroquois tribal elders, "we must consider the impact of our decision on the next seven generations."

I put these two props up on the podium and tell the audience, "These are two very different ways of looking at our purpose in life. One is 'The earth is doomed. Let's drink.' The other is 'We are responsible for generations yet to come. Let's make wise choices. Let's live as good ancestors as those before us chose to do.'" Whether or not you have children, you can make choices with those who will come after you on this planet in mind.

What really separates us from other species is that we are uniquely capable of living on two levels, the present and the future. We can make choices, and we can make those choices based not on what is best in the moment, but on what is best for those we will never know, generations from now. And here's some good news. The happiest people are those who know they are living lives that have meaning beyond themselves. If you want to feel fulfilled—really, truly fulfilled—then live beyond your own life. Live as a good ancestor to those you will never know. We are at our best when we know for certain that we have transcended our own brief and beautiful time on earth. That is the essence of being fully human. That is the essence of what it means to lead a meaningful life.

Death means little if it is not impetus to change ourselves while we are alive and thereby the future when we are gone. We need not be trapped in yesterday's ways. A little red velvet dress with white lace. My dead father's prayer shawl upon my shoulders. Each of us is here only because of the loving choices made by those who walked before us—the choices of good ancestors. When our bodies have long returned to the earth and our souls are but a whisper, will the same be said of us? What memories will we leave as our legacy?

When my dad lost his mind to Alzheimer's, he forgot who he was and who those who loved him were. In a sense, that forgetting meant that for him, neither he nor we existed any longer. A new he and a new we were created in the vacuum of his mind; nothing was the same.

That is, unless and until I chose to make use of the most precious of all gifts—my memories. In order to bring my father back to life, all I had to do was remember all those simple things that he loved. Unlike other dads, he didn't know or care about sports or hobbies or new gadgets. My dad taught me to love nature, fishing, pancakes, corned beef hash, and Mom's soups. Mostly Dad taught me to enjoy a moment during that very moment.

Sooner or later our hearts are broken by death. Sure, we put on our masks of normalcy and walk out into the world day after day, but then just the right moment—the exact place or smell or taste or image—arrives to remind us of how deeply we miss those we love who are gone. The grief cuts sharply at first. Then a dull ache sets in that never, ever goes away entirely until we are asleep; even then, cruelly and delightfully, our loved ones are there to speak to us.

They speak to us at the anniversary of their deaths, at the wedding when they are not there to dance, on their birthday, on ours, at the Thanksgiving table with an empty chair, an empty place in our hearts. They speak to us and we miss them. They are the absence that is forever present.

I have seen nearly a thousand corpses, more than enough to know that a body is not a person. It is a vessel. There is so much more to us than our physical presence. Where does the soul go? I do not know. But I have heard too many stories, real stories, to dismiss the possibility of an afterlife. My wife's best friend, Laura, died fifteen years ago. Every year on Laura's birthday, Betsy sees a ladybug. Perhaps it's just a coincidence. Perhaps it is just a projection. But perhaps not.

My friend Lorin, whose husband, Eddie, died in my arms after a seven-year battle with brain cancer, told me this story. "At one of my grief group meetings, we had to go around and answer the question: 'If you had to say one thing to your spouse right now, what would it be?' I said, 'Please, keep showing me signs you are here with me.' I returned to my car. Out of the hundreds of songs in my iTunes library, Springsteen's 'The Promised Land' started playing, the one song Eddie had told me he wanted played at his funeral."

These stories fill me with warmth, hope, and strength. Dreams, butterflies, ladybugs, a smell, a vision, a song, a soft breeze in a hard moment—these reminders are real and are to be treasured. They are their own afterlife. They are the beauty of what remains.

I believe the dead are present in so many ways. They live in ways that we who ache know all too well—some sweet, some bitter. And whether they are our own projection or some deliberate force of their own matters not, at least not to those of us who miss them. Whether only from within us or perhaps from elsewhere, what matters is that they do come to chat with us now and then.

Years ago, while leafing through one of my wife's magazines, I read a beautiful story about Caitlin, a stay-at-home mom who'd had a few run-ins with her own mother recently that had given her reason to pause.

Yesterday my mother told me to skip a step in a recipe, which turned out to be very good advice. Last week, she told me to sit down and have a sandwich and a glass of juice before going to a meeting. Again, right on the money. My mom is always telling me what to do in her bossy, good-hearted way. I always do just what she tells me and I never talk back.

The reason I don't is that she is dead and I am not. As anyone with a dead loved one knows, the dead have the ability to come through loud and clear when they feel like it.

Like not so long ago, when my big sister and I were clearing out our mother's kitchen. Mom, you see, had recently died, taking with her a lifetime of family secrets as well as her recipe for Apple Betty. I pulled open a cupboard and found inside it her old Pyrex measuring cup. I took it in my hand, and for the first time in my life, I really looked at it. And that was when I realized that all of the red measuring lines had completely faded away. In that moment, I realized that the woman I had once made cry by returning to college early one winter break had cooked me so many pancakes and chocolate diamond cookies that her Pyrex measuring cup had been worn clean.

Some of those meals I had eaten cheerfully, some sullenly, and many I had eaten without so much as a word of thanks. I stood in my mother's kitchen looking at that measuring cup and I thought, Now I am a person with a broken heart. . . . [My sister] was standing right next to me and she said, "I take it you're keeping the cup?"

"Yes," I said weakly. And she put a red sticker on it and set it on top of the stack of things to be sent to my house. At home, I unwrapped the cup and set it prominently on the kitchen windowsill, where it was to become the centerpiece of the year's long meditation on grief.

But it was hard to keep my mind on mourning. My children, for example, kept asking for pancakes and Spanish rice and trips to the playground and they kept needing their shoes tied. In fact, tying their shoes became like a part-time job. I began to imagine a day when my own children are all grown up and going through my possessions after my death. What if they come across an old shoelace in a drawer and begin sobbing about all the times I tied their shoes and they had run off without even saying thank you? What if they become seized with guilt? How delicious.

But not to be encouraged, I will have to do my own bit of talking from beyond the grave.

"Patrick and Connor," I'll say, "tying those shoelaces is why I had you." And then right after that I'll probably say, "By the way, why don't you both sit down and have a sandwich and maybe a nice glass of juice?"

Caitlin is right. The dead do speak. Those we love and have lost do speak. They speak to us through a Pyrex measuring cup, through our own children, through dreams, through their kindness we sometimes did not fully appreciate until relived and retold from the grave. There is a life after death for those we love—a life lived in our hearts and souls, dreams and daily life.

But there is even more. Our loved ones not only speak to us—they see through us. "They sit," as the poet Rabindranath Tagore put it, "in the pupils of your eyes."

In one case, a loved one now gone literally dwells in the pupil of his wife's eyes. In the *Los Angeles Times,* Valerie Reitman reported about a man named Richard Meza, who had been planning to retire in June 2006. He and his wife, LoAnn, met in a college English class. Married twenty-four years, they were going to move from the city to a house they were building on ten acres in rural Virginia.

A "serious cat lover," . . . Richard had been feeding strays, as he often did, . . . when he was shot. When police arrived—

alerted by someone who had heard the gunshots—Meza was dead.

No arrest has been made.

Richard Meza had often joked to his wife and friends that he should give her one of his corneas. . . . LoAnn Meza could no longer see well enough to drive to the grocery store, which she said greatly troubled her husband. The vision in her left eye had been deteriorating for about 15 years after complications from a procedure intended to cure near-sightedness. . . .

A neighbor paying her a condolence call . . . reminded her of her husband's wish. At the insistence of the friend, LoAnn Meza got in touch with . . . the Jules Stein Eye Institute. By then, the one-week window on cornea viability for transplant after a donor's death was nearly up. [The operation] was performed that evening.

The next day [the doctor] removed LoAnn's eye patch. Though looking somber and worn, she said in a videotape of the procedure, "I'm so happy. This is a miracle in my life—to have my vision back."

LoAnn literally sees the world through her husband's eyes. Can we all do figuratively for our loved ones what modern medicine enabled this woman to do literally for her husband? Isn't that the challenge for all of us who have lost people we love—to keep them alive, to enable them to speak to us from a measuring cup or a breeze, a smell, a taste, a dream; to let them see, really see life, and to live life through us?

See it, see it all for them. The bride and groom lifted high in chairs, their young faces full of terror, promise, and love. See it, see it all for them. The grandchildren growing and graduating, struggling and succeeding. The soccer games and goals, the games won and lost, the report cards, the Thanksgiving table—sweet potatoes and pecan pie, bickering and bittersweet goodbyes—the candles burning brightly with family all around, a perfect fall day, a cloudless azure sky, and sun shining on the sage-colored hills. Ocean waves and soaring birds. See it, see it all for them. You who mourn lost loves, let them dwell in the pupils of your eyes, let them live in memory.

Be prepared for not only how sweet but also how bitter memory can be. I never realized it until my father died, but the truth is, there is a lot more to memory than laughter and love. All these months after viewing him in a plain pine casket—cold and dead—I want to forget that image of my dad. I can't. Months after shoveling earth onto that same casket with a thunk, I want to forget that sound. I can't. "I don't want to remember. I don't want to remember. I don't want to remember," I tell myself. Yet I cannot forget the ugliness or the surreal power of his death.

And if Freud was even partially right, there is a world of memories not about my dad's death but about his life that, try as I may, I can only sort of forget. He was flawed. I once attended a lecture by a world-renowned scholar of Yiddish. After his remarks, he called on audience members for questions. I told him that I wanted my children to learn Yiddish, but I did not want to perpetuate the racism, xenophobia, sexism, and anti-Christian sentiments that were so much a part of the language of my youth—my father's secret family code. I wanted to know if there was any way to reconcile this conflict. The professor was surprised by my question. He responded that Yiddish was an extremely elevated language, that Shakespeare has been translated into Yiddish. And then he suggested that my negative associations with the values transmitted in Yiddish were the product of whoever taught me Yiddish, not the language itself. Yiddish is not racist, xenophobic, sexist, and anti-Christian, my dad was.

I hold many harsh memories of discipline and anger, anxiety, and fear repressed and banished to the basement of my subconscious, constantly pounding on that same basement ceiling with a broomstick, reverberating in ways mysterious and dark in the core of my conscious life, animating my own flaws, dysfunction, and vulnerabilities. That is the secret truth of memory: we summon it, yet it controls us. It is exquisite, and it hurts—like being caressed and spat on at the same time.

Whenever a villain is mentioned in classical rabbinic literature, his name is followed by an acronym for the words "May his name be blotted out." In the minds of the ancient rabbis, the worst thing one could wish upon another, the curse of curses, was that he or she be forgotten.

And yet within that very curse the name of the villain is actually perpetuated. We can wish that evil, sadness, and ugliness be forgotten, but saying, "Don't think about it," involves thinking about it—an attempt at squaring a circle; a fruitless, impossible denial of the constant that is memory itself. When George Santayana said, "Those who cannot remember the past are condemned to repeat it," he was only half right. For it is also true that those who *only* remember the past, who do nothing about it, are also doomed to repeat it. If my father's flaws were all I ever learned about how to live as a husband and a father, the cycle would never be broken. This is the trap of memory that causes so much pain in so many families.

I often counsel people to forgive the sins of those who have died, who did in life the best they could, and who, if they knew the pain they had caused, would have been truly sorry for what they had done. More times than not, people know they should forgive but say they just can't. "Rabbi, you have no idea what she did. How she hurt me. How she cut me down. How she turned her back on me when I needed her most. I want to forgive, but it's too hard." Long ago I learned that what the unforgiving are often really saying is not that it is impossible to forgive, but that it is impossible to forget. We have no choice but to remember pain, the same way we have no choice when we are asked not to think about a pink elephant, but far worse. Such is the grip of memory. It is a force unlike any other in our lives.

When a good person dies, a different wish is suggested when his name is mentioned; a beautiful wish: "May his memory be a blessing." Seemingly different, these two aphorisms, "May his name be blotted out" and "May his memory be a blessing," speak the same truth—to be remembered is to live beyond the grave in ways terrible and sublime.

How else can we hold on to the people we love, to the past that defines us, to the offenses that wound us, or to the laughter and the love that warm us? How else can we hold on to anything in a world whose centrifuge of speed and stress tries to whirl us all apart? What else can I do when I miss my dad so much? Nothing, other than embrace this blessing, this curse, this imperfect gift, this burden, this holy vessel: memory.

In the eulogy I wrote for my father, I tried to hold on to everything:

In a word, Dad was frugal. He rinsed paper plates, laid them out to dry, and reused them. Instead of paying three dollars for tea, he asked the waitress for a little hot water, then pulled a nasty old tea bag from home out of the pocket of a flannel shirt from Marshalls that had so many colors in it, he looked like a flag from a foreign country. And the pièce de résistance—he reused his dental floss.

This behavior was the result of a world view, a philosophical doctrine often articulated to us in our youth with a Yiddish phrase that had the status of the Torah in our house: A bissel aun a bissle vert a full schissel, *which means "A little and a little fills the container." I know, it sounds much better in Yiddish.*

To my dad, a little was a lot. He grew up a skinny kid on public assistance and married Mom at eighteen. They had five kids before they were thirty and no safety net if he failed. There was a reason he wasted nothing and reminded us again and again that a little was a lot. He appreciated small things: A nice piece of fruit, which of course tasted so much better if it was stolen from someone else's tree. A slice from a perfect avocado. A sunny day. Hank Williams and Johnny Cash. A joke, the dirtier the better. Watching All in the Family *in his vibrating Naugahyde chair, peeling an orange into a perfect spiral before handing out slices to each of us one at a time as if we were a nest full of hungry birds.*

He was crude—and hilarious. One look at a guy and Dad could sum him up with a single perfect Yiddish word: schmuck, chazer *(pig),* bayshick *(idiot),* putz *(a lot like a* schmuck*),* fresser *(a big eater—a lot like a* chazer*),* gonif *(crook),* schlucha *(slut),* chochem *(wise guy),* schlepper *(bum), or worse, a* schmutzig schlepper *(dirty bum)! And he could encapsulate an entire family's ethos with a simple* "fineh menschen," *which literally means "refined people," but in Dad's sarcastic lexicon meant precisely the opposite.*

And yet, as harsh as his judgments could be, and that was pretty harsh, Dad had a very large soft spot for the down and out. When he saw others in trouble, he would look at them and say, "It's a zuch en vie*"—a terrible kind of hurt. He gave them jobs. He lent them money. He was their friend. Everyone borrowed money from Dad. He helped all of us at one time or another and he never, ever held it over us. When we really needed someone to rescue us, Dad showed up and he was fierce in his love.*

Dad was as loyal a friend as a person could be. His buddies were lifelong. Greg Super, Paul Serber, Henry Nosek, Harry Sack (a name we laughed about a lot as kids), Joey Polanski, Joey Garber, and his newest but dear, dear friend Robert—who was so much more than a caregiver to Dad. Robert, you are the only person on earth who is both a saint

*and an honorary Jew. God bless you for the dignity and hap-
piness you brought to Dad's life.*

*I've officiated at a lot of funerals—many hundreds. And
when I sit with families to prepare, it's almost never the person's résumé we end up talking about. It's the little things, and
it was the little things that I learned from Dad that have
actually loomed largest in my life.*

*I watched him work at Leder Brothers, outside in the cold,
outside in the heat, covered in grease with purple fingernails
from smashing his fingers between some pipes. He worked so
hard. And Mom knew, because of his unceasing effort and
strength, that she and her five children would always be se-
cure. And no, he wasn't like the other dads who knew about
baseball and wore suits and ties. But he could back up a semi
and run a crane. He was so, so tough—ten years he gutted out
his disease. It took so much from him, and yet somehow, he
found a way to smile whenever one of us walked in the room.*

*The last real conversation I remember having with Dad
before thinking became hard work and confusing for him was
about my fundraising for the temple. Mom was there too. We
were sitting around that Formica table in the Palm Springs
kitchen where they sat together for all those years drinking
countless pots of tea from the stainless-steel thermal container
and playing countless rounds of Rummikub, with Dad think-*

ing and thinking while Mom would yell, "Oy, Leonard, krutz a chus (scratch an itch) already." It was at that table Dad asked, "How's work going?" And I told him, feeling a little sorry for myself, that it was really hard to raise all the money we needed, and I wasn't sure I could do it. He looked at me, smiled, and said, "Az m'schtuptis, gatis"—If you push, it goes. Remember, almost everything Dad said was a double entendre. So he wasn't just talking about fundraising. That was Dad. Simple, funny, and right. Whatever your goal, just keep pushing. Dad taught me every day of his life to hit harder and longer and more brutally than anyone if I wanted to win. It has made me who I am.

He didn't care about sports or hobbies or new gadgets like other dads. He hated phonies. He taught us all to beware of them. Never once did I see him covet a single material thing unless it was cheap and he could eat it. He taught us to love nature and fishing, Town Talk pancakes, Lincoln Del corned beef hash, and Mom's soups. Mom fed Dad like her life depended on it. And frankly, it did. If whatever came to the table was met with a "To be honest, honey, it don't do nothing for me," a dark, cold cloud descended upon Decatur Lane. Mostly Dad taught me to enjoy a moment during that moment. So many times when he was eating something delicious and plenty of it, or we were walking in the sunshine somewhere beautiful, he would just look around and ask rhetorically, "Are we livin'?"

And in those moments he would remind us that life was a fargenign—a pleasure.

Nothing brought him more pleasure than his family. He loved being Papa to Matt, Mike, Lissy, Andrew, Lindsay, Ethan, Eli, Aaron, Hannah, and Elliot. Ah, those field trips with Grandma and Papa in that brown Oldsmobile the size of an aircraft carrier. Sitting on those beaded seat covers, Papa at the helm, off to the Anza-Borrego Desert to see the wildflowers and buy some dollar-a-bag grapefruit. He taught you how to drink tea, how to comparison-shop for a laser pointer, and that if you don't brush your teeth, you're gonna get dingle berries. And of course how to do a mitzvah. Let me explain.

Lissy was a young girl visiting Grandma and Papa in Palm Springs. She calls her mom to report on the previous day's adventures and tells Marilyn that the previous night, when it got dark, Papa told her to put on black clothes. Off they drove to the empty parking lot by the bank down the street, where there was a big Meyer lemon tree that had dropped bags' worth of lemons on the ground. In the dark, Papa and Lissy, dressed in black, bagged up all those fallen lemons, and plenty from off the tree too, I am sure, then drove home with their loot in the trunk. Papa explained to Lissy the lemon tree caper was actually a mitzvah to keep people from tripping on lemons the next day.

Dementia stole Dad's memory, but it has sharpened mine. It has helped me remember who he really was, long before the shared remembrances of today. For years we have tried to remember him as he was—every lesson, every joke and gesture. Sundays at the roller rink, watching Mom and him glide and dance on wheels, savoring those few happy, graceful moments. How he worked so hard for so long, and the way he loved butter brickle ice cream on a hot summer night. His forgetting disease taught me to remember so many tiny, beautiful things. The last years have been a lesson in essentialism, a stripping away—leaving behind the sweetest man that was always at Dad's core.

You were so right, Dad. "A bissel aun a bissle vert a full schissel." *Our hearts will be full forever with the beauty of what remains.*

Make It Beautiful

As the father has mercy on his children,
so must the son have mercy on the forlorn soul of his father.
—JACOB HOROWITZ

My mother is mostly absent from this book. I feel bad about it. "That's because your father claimed you as his when you were very young," my psychiatrist matter-of-factly observed. He was right. I was my father's *kaddishlah*, a Yiddish term of endearment, like *mamelah* or *bubbalah*, given to the firstborn son upon whom it would be incumbent, according to Jewish law, to say the mourner's Kaddish prayer when his father died. In the most traditional, superstitious sense, without a kaddishlah, one's soul might well be in jeopardy. My dad loved my three older sisters and my younger brother, but I, his firstborn son, was singled out. He wasn't religious enough to know what kaddishlah meant, but somehow he knew that his legacy would be my responsibility in ways different from my siblings. For better and for worse, he felt a special obligation to prepare me for the role I was born to fulfill—the spiritual, emotional, and physical duties incumbent upon me when Alzheimer's caused him to slowly disappear in plain sight for a decade until he died, and in a sense, the responsibility for the destiny of his soul thereafter.

A developer friend of mine who hires a lot of kids coming out of college and trade school said to me not long ago, "People who scrubbed toilets at some point in their youth tend to do pretty well in business." I thought of my dad, of the smell of Pine-Sol mixed with hot water in a metal bucket; the way it chapped my hands with each dunk of the stiff brush and the way my seven-year-old knees hurt after a day of scrubbing floors and toilets at the junkyard; all preparation to be Lenny Leder's kaddishlah.

My dad worked hard his entire childhood. He was the kid who left school at noon every day because he had to work at the dump my grandfather owned. It was there he and my uncle, mere boys, picked the tin cans out of other people's garbage, took them to a junkyard, and pocketed a few pennies to help their family. A decade ago I went on a two-week mission to India, during which I spent time in the slums of Mumbai: a jumbled mass of shacks stacked upon one another, with raw sewage in the trenches of the dirt paths, and a sea of stinking, rat-infested garbage for literally as far as my eyes could see.

Many of the children in the Mumbai slums spend their days rummaging through that garbage for anything salvageable. Those hapless children of the untouchables are called ragpickers. When I gazed upon that vast sea of rot and refuse, I thought to myself, if my father had been born here, he would have been among the ragpickers. What is the difference, really, between rags in Mumbai and tin cans in Minneapolis?

I was scrubbing toilets as a boy because in one particular way, my father wanted my childhood, wanted me, to be just like him. Whatever he learned from the dump, he wanted me to know too. So I too worked hard as a child—toilets, urinals, and greasy floors were my classroom. That experience has enabled me again and again to do the dirty work of the rabbinate and to outlast and overcome the obstacles in front of me. I can stay up until sunrise to finish a sermon, cajole the wealthy, officiate at fourteen funerals in seventeen days, be on call nearly all the time, run a large institution without ever really being able to show anger, run a sort of mental health clinic on my couch of tears, on occasion work for and with people who are egotistical and insecure—none of it stops me because I was my dad's disciple, and his real religion was hard work.

I hated my father's harshness, but it gave me the strength to create the life I have led. I told him as much during that visit to the nursing home when I felt that he soon would no longer be able to understand me. I told him that he had given me everything I needed to succeed because he taught me to work hard. I said it had made all the difference. I told him he was a great dad. He stared back for the briefest of moments, looked down and away, and wiped his eyes. I hope he felt what I wanted him to feel, what I needed him to feel, for him and for me: understood, acquitted, forgiven.

Other than bequeathing me a brutal work ethic, in many ways my father wanted to be sure my life would not be like his. Part of him longed to be the little boy who could have been spared the harshness and deprivation of his childhood, and that yearning resulted in the things he did to give me what he never had in order for me to become what he could never be. I don't know how much of his effort to make up for the deficits of his own youth was conscious; I think most of it was not. Either way, the kid who had to leave school at noon, who had one pair of pants for work and one for everything else, who was mocked by his ignorant, abusive parents with the words "Look at the professor" when he came home with a book, raised all five of his children with the mantra "There is always money for books," sent me to summer camp, college, Europe, and grad school so that I could someday write books. Man, did he and we make up for the literal hunger of his childhood with a lot of good food over a lot of years. After more than two years of mourning, I realize so clearly that my father's mission was for me to become what he could not.

When I was a boy of twelve studying for my bar mitzvah three days a week at the synagogue, my dad sometimes picked me up on his way home from work. Often, we would stay for the late afternoon service held each weekday for those who needed to say the mourner's Kaddish for a loved one now gone. Sometimes my dad volunteered to lead the brief service, nearly all in English save the most rudimentary Hebrew prayers. As my bar mitzvah date approached and it was his turn to lead one afternoon, my dad turned to me and said, "Why don't you lead today? Start here." I never felt more like a man.

A decade later, during my senior year of college, I told my father I was applying to the seminary. "Rabbis are beggars" was his response. My dad had a full measure of disdain for anyone who was not self-made. And in his own crude way, he was right. The most difficult and distasteful thing I have ever done as a rabbi is raise money. Some of those I courted were gracious, kind, and generous, but others, far less so. When I look back at it now, maybe my dad wasn't so much trying to discourage me as to warn me. After all, a decade before, on that seemingly ordinary day, he had handed me that prayer book and helped me in the most crucial way any parent can help a child—with the words "Start here." Did he understand what he was doing that day—the path he set me on? I do not know. What I *do* know is that he gave me everything I needed to walk my path with passion, sacrifice, and honor.

Of course, for those of us who do and especially for those of us who do not have children, there are so many other important ways to achieve a legacy beyond the transfer of unfulfilled aspirations from parent to child. Did you mentor others at work? Did you write, sing, dance, play, build, feed, inspire, teach, or just plain do right by others? I have worked hard to lead, create, write, speak, and share the brilliance of the sages. I have cared for many when they were most frightened and vulnerable and when they were experiencing their greatest moments of joy. These too are important legacies separate from being the son of my father and the father of two children.

Yet, in my case, no matter what else I have become, I am mostly my father's son, evidenced in the way I worked when other kids played, fearing the wrath of my father for not having done my best. He taught me the importance of thrift and a love of good food. We share crude laughs and an impatience with fools. From him I gained a love for wildflowers and sun-dappled water, the oaks turning golden in the fall and the lilacs that magically seemed to blossom in our Minnesota backyard each year on my dad's birthday, causing him to remark, "God is the best florist." He was rough and uneducated, but my dad awakened me to spirituality from the ground up in a very powerful way. He still makes me laugh a lot, especially when I know the exact Yiddish word he would have used to sum up the person or situation in front of me. More than anyone, my wonderful and flawed dad prepared me to carry on a legacy.

I am sure my father had no idea the Talmud says, "The son acquits the father." But I hope with all my heart that is true of me. For a child to acquit a parent requires more than mindlessly perpetuating an inherited set of habits or values. The older I become and the more distanced from my father's life and death, the more I realize how incumbent it is upon us all to make the legacy we inherit more beautiful and more authentically our own, not only by living as our loved ones lived in their finest moments, but also by choosing what not to carry forth from their worst.

The Bible, for example, is full of stories that are hard to justify at face value: Cain killing his brother Abel out of jealousy; Abraham banishing his mistress and his son Ishmael to die in the desert and then preparing to sacrifice his other son, Isaac, binding him to a pyre and raising a knife to slit his throat; Jacob deceiving his blind father into mistakenly granting him the family's birthright blessing; Joseph's brothers selling him into slavery and telling their father (the same Jacob who deceived his own father) that his beloved son was dead. How do we justify or understand so much dysfunction in a book revered by billions for almost three thousand years? To me, there is only one answer, and it is very simple. Often the Bible, like the people we love and the family we are born into, teaches us by negative example how not to behave.

Imagine a beautiful marble statue and consider for a moment how that statue began. It was born out of a solid block of stone shaped by a sculptor who artfully removed, chiseled chip by chiseled chip, everything from that block that was not beautiful. Creating by removing to reveal the beauty that was always hidden within is how I choose to think of my life as I slowly became a man, a husband, and a father in the shadow of my father, and even more so in his slow decline and in the aftermath of his life. To be hard-working without being punishing. To raise my children without fear of harm from me. To tuck them in at night and read to them; to be there for the plays, the recitals, and the games; to play catch with them. To live with greater respect for women and less respect for ridicule; to fear poverty less, all while still embracing the glory of nature, a good laugh, an outstretched arm to a friend, something delicious—a counting of our many blessings, which is what my dad meant when he asked rhetorically, "Are we livin'?"

To a man who reached out to her after losing his young son in a car accident, the author Cheryl Strayed wrote: "The fact is that pain teaches us things. It shows us shades and hues we could not otherwise see. It requires us to suffer. It compels us to reach. Your son was your greatest gift in his life and he is your greatest gift in his death too. Receive it. Let your dead boy be your most profound revelations. Create something of him. Make it beautiful." The beauty of what remains is neither passive nor accidental. We create it through the deliberate choices we make—chiseled chip by chiseled chip.

If life is good, then death must be bad is the way most people think, but this isn't really so. I am not for a moment trying to make sense of the death of a child or anyone who has not been granted his or her full measure of life. But generally speaking, is more really better or is there something about death that defines the essence of life itself? In his essay "L'Chaim and Its Limits: Why Not Immortality?" Leon Kass put it this way: "To argue that human life would be better without death is to argue that human life would be better being something other than human."

Why? Why is death preferable to immortality? Because without death, to what would we aspire? Could life be serious or meaningful without mortality? Could life be beautiful? "Death," says Wallace Stevens, "is the mother of beauty." The beauty of flowers depends on the fact that they soon wither. How deeply could one deathless "human" being really love another? It is the simple fact that we do not have forever that makes our love for each other so profound. And, without death, would there be such a thing as a moral life? To know that we will die means we must stand for something greater than ourselves in life. It is death that makes us human in the best sense of that word.

. . .

When my father was clearly reaching the last year or two of his life, my mother started offering me his things each time I visited. I almost always said no thanks. There was very little of the material world that would help me hold on to a dad who never cared much about things. One day, just as it was time for me to leave her and fly home to Los Angeles, she reached into a drawer and handed me my father's prayer shawl, called a tallis in Hebrew. "Here," she said, emotionless, showing me yet again that she had left him long before he died. "Take Dad's tallis, he doesn't need it." I was quiet, brokenhearted, and profoundly moved as I held the slightly stained, cream-colored fabric with muted blue stripes in my hands. My dad's tallis was mine. There was nothing else she needed to say. He really was going to die, and much of what would remain of him would rest upon my shoulders. Much like that moment decades ago when my father handed me that prayer book, I felt like a man in a way I never had before.

When I got back to Los Angeles, I took the tallis to the dry cleaner. "What's this?" asked the Filipino man who had been taking in my shirts and suits for nearly twenty years.

"It's special to my family," I said. "It belonged to my dad and I wear it when I pray. Can you clean it?"

"Yeah, sure. Pick it up next week."

When I returned for the tallis, the same man handed it to

me with a tense look on his face and an apology on his lips. The blue stripes had bled into the cream-colored fabric and the entire tallis was frayed. Through years of improper storage and a dry cleaner who apparently had never seen a tallis before, I was left with a blurred, frayed semblance of what was. *It figures*, I thought to myself. *My dad is blurred and frayed, and now his tallis is too.*

I wear that tallis on the holiest evening of each year—the one that mimics death and impels us toward forgiveness. The shawl is perfect in its imperfection, a reminder that even the most fortunate among us are impermanent, our legacies eventually carried forth by others. Death and memory have smoothed the sharp edges of being my father's son. My bitterness gone, I understand now that my entire life he was preparing me, trusting me with his soul; a soul now acquitted in my heart. I understand that we really don't have forever, we really can't have it all, and we take nothing with us when we leave. But what we leave behind, no matter how blurred and frayed, can be beautiful. Often it strikes me, exquisitely, achingly, that I really love my dad.

Despite burying a thousand people, I never thought very deeply about my own death until my father died. It wasn't until I saw him lifeless in that coffin that it occurred to me in an inescapable, matter-of-fact, undeniable, and self-evident way, I too will die. I really am going to die. It is so . . . simple.

And it has caused me to think very deeply about how I want to live and upon whose shoulders my soul shall someday rest. I often hope and wonder, will I be acquitted?

I am finishing this book on my sixtieth birthday. Sixty years ago to the day, my father first held me in his arms and likely wondered what would become of his firstborn son. I imagine him thinking, *How shall I make him mine? How can I spare him the pain of my own youth? How can I help him make real what I could only dream of?* In the midst of my musing, my thirty-one-year-old son, Aaron, who was quarantining with us during the pandemic, bounded down the stairs and said, "Hey, Dad, look what I found." He had been cleaning out his childhood room, and there they were, our old baseball mitts. The sight of them transported me back two decades to endless hours of tossing the ball back and forth until dark with my sweet freckle-faced boy. We took the mitts and went into the backyard for our first game of catch in fifteen years. We felt again the simple pleasure of the back-and-forth, caught up in the rhythm and smack of the ball as it hit the well-worn leather pocket of our gloves. We said nothing—my kaddish-lah and I—silently embracing the beauty of what would someday remain.

ACKNOWLEDGMENTS

At its truest, gratitude is not a momentary impulse, but a way of life. I will be grateful for the rest of my life to the many people who have made this book possible. My teachers throughout the years, my mother and siblings, my colleagues and the families of Wilshire Boulevard Temple who trust me with their stories and their hearts. To my friend Margot Schupf, who believed in me and gave me entreé to the community of agents, editors, and publishers who define the very heights of publishing in America. Margot led me to my wonderful agent, friend, and Buddhist enlightener Stephanie Tade, who in turn brought me and this project to the extraordinary Caroline Sutton at Penguin Random House, who had me at "hello." Caroline inspired me to find the book within me she knew was hiding in plain sight, bestowing upon me one of the most profound gifts of my life. To Stephanie Higgs, who saw the same potential within the manuscript and helped me create the architecture to make it real, thank you. To Gretchen van Nuys for her assistance with the tedium of permissions, to Nancy Inglis for her excellent copyediting, and to Hannah Steigmeyer and Natasha Soto for making sure every publishing detail was attended to, my sincere thanks as well.

I have no words to describe the love I feel for my wife, Betsy, and our children, Aaron and Hannah, but hope somehow I manage to live it and say it every day. And finally, to my dad, who has taught me as much in death as he did in life about the beauty of what remains.

PERMISSIONS CREDITS

Also by Steve Leder